In Search of Better Angels

This book is dedicated to my son Lincoln,
and to my daughters Allison and Sallie
With love as you create your own stories,
Dad

Stories of Disability in the Human Family

In Search of Better Angels

J. DAVID SMITH

CORWIN PRESS, INC.
A Sage Publications Company
Thousand Oaks, California

For information:

Corwin Press, Inc.
A Sage Publications Company
2455 Teller Road
Thousand Oaks, California 91320
www.corwinpress.com

Sage Publications Ltd.
6 Bonhill Street
London EC2A 4PU
United Kingdom

Sage Publications India Pvt. Ltd.
B-42, Panchsheel Enclave
Post Box 4109
New Delhi 110 017 India

Printed in the United States of America

Library of Congress Cataloging-in-Publication Data

Smith, J. David, 1944-
In search of better angels: Stories of disability in the human family /
J. David Smith.
         p. cm.
Includes bibliographical references and index.
ISBN 0-7619-3840-0 (Cloth)
ISBN 0-7619-3841-9 (Paper)
     1. Children with disabilities—Education. 2. Inclusive education. 3. Children with disabilities—Care—History. I. Title: Stories of disability in the human family.
II. Title.
LC4019.S55 2003
371.9-dc21

                                    2003001715

This book is printed on acid-free paper.

03   04   05   06   10 9 8 7 6 5 4 3 2 1

Acquisitions Editor:	Robert D. Clouse
Associate Editor:	Kristen L. Gibson
Editorial Assistant:	Jingle Vea
Copy Editor:	Jamie Robinson
Typesetter:	C&M Digitals (P) Ltd.
Indexer:	Kathy Paparchontis
Cover Designer:	Tracy E. Miller
Production Artist:	Lisa Miller

Contents

Preface

In Search of Better Angels is a book about the challenges and possibilities we face in creating a more inclusive and welcoming society for children and adults with disabilities. It is about understanding and celebrating human diversity. It is also a book about the commonality of needs and aspirations throughout the human family.

The values expressed in this book are symbolized in the title by the image of "better angels." I borrowed this symbol from Abraham Lincoln's first inaugural address. He closed his address to the Union that was torn and filled with anger with an appeal to "the better angels of our nature." He hoped that the better angels in America would lead to peace and solidarity.

I believe that the creation of more inclusive society for all people depends on calling upon the "better angels" of our character. It depends, as well, on our true commitment to the ideals of human equality and a democratic society.

ACKNOWLEDGMENTS

Thanks go to those of you who may read this book and know you were there when I needed enlightenment, encouragement, and confirmation. Thank you for caring for me and about my work.

Much of the credit for all of my work as a scholar belongs to Joyce Smith and our children Lincoln, Allison, and Sallie. Their love has sustained me in all that I have attempted over the decades. They have brought the greatest richness to my life.

Darlene Moore and Peggy Ward have blessed this book with their care and attention. Each gave her genuine concern to the quality and integrity of the preparation of the manuscript. They are cherished friends and

Note: Earlier versions of some of the chapters of this book were published in *Mental Retardation* and *Remedial and Special Education,* and in the author's book *Inclusion: Schools for All Students.*

colleagues. My thanks also goto Robin Patterson and Alison Mitchell for their loyal and competent research assistance.

Finally, my deepest appreciation goes to the men, women, and children whose stories have become part of this book. Most important to me is that their stories have become part of my life.

In addition, Corwin Press would like to gratefully acknowledge the contributions of the following reviewers:

David Grapka
Project Coordinator, Technology Resources
    for Education (T.R.E.) Center
New York Council of Administrators of
    Special Education, Albany, NY

W. David Mills
Section Chief, Exceptional Children's Division
North Carolina Department of Public Instruction, Raleigh, NC

Lee Nielsen
Teacher, Los Angeles Unified School District
Woodland Hills, CA

Leonard O. Pellicer
Dean, School of Education
University of La Verne, La Verne, CA

Jolinda Simes
District Mentor for Special Education
Minneapolis Public Schools, Minneapolis, MN

About the Author

J. David Smith is Provost and Senior Vice Chancellor at The University of Virginia's College at Wise. He earned both baccalaureate and graduate degrees from Virginia Commonwealth University. He was awarded a second master's degree and his doctorate from Columbia University. His professional experience includes work as a public school teacher and as a counselor. He and his wife, Joyce, served two years in Jamaica working as Peace Corps volunteers. Before coming to The University of Virginia's College at Wise as Provost, he served as Dean of the School of Education and Human Services at Longwood University. He also served as Chair of the Department of Educational Psychology at the University of South Carolina. He began his higher education career at Lynchburg College. Smith has made numerous invited presentations to national and international audiences and regularly contributes to the professional literature on education, human services, and public policy through journal articles. He is the author of ten books. One of the integrating themes of his research and writing has been a concern for the rights and dignity of people with disabilities. Smith has devoted much of his scholarship to the study of the history of eugenics and its impact on social and educational policy, and he has also been active in addressing contemporary problems and issues in education.

Introduction

Power and Epiphany:
Reflections on the Personal
and Cultural Value of Disabilities

The uses and abuses of power are fundamental concerns of the human condition. Most of us are aware that the challenge of encouraging good and preventing destructive uses of power has been a prevailing theme of history. It is also central to the most compelling issues we face today. Less obvious to many of us, however, is the question of how the actions and values associated with power may be influenced by people who are thought of as lacking power themselves. The stories in this introduction are offered as a way of establishing the context for the book that follows. They provide insights into the transforming influence of children and adults with disabilities on the lives of others. They are profiles of the "power of the powerless."

The Aryan Nations, a Cleft Palate, and an Epiphany

In 1992, Floyd Cochran was the chief recruiter for the Aryan Nations. As the fifth-ranking leader of this self-proclaimed neo-Nazi, white supremacist organization, he was admired for his skill in dealing effectively with the public and a critical press. Cochran was very successful in using his media savvy and marketing skills to attract young people to the organization. He became the group's national spokesperson and was described by the Aryan Nations' chief, the Reverend Richard Butler, as being destined to be "the next Goebbels" (Hochschild, 1994, p. 29). In July of that year, however, Floyd Cochran was suddenly ordered off the Nations' compound. The Reverend Butler gave him five minutes to leave.

1

The rift in Cochran's relationship with the Aryan Nations had begun earlier that year. Shortly before he was to speak at the Hitler Youth Festival in Idaho, Cochran mentioned to the Nations' security chief that he was running late because he had been talking with his wife on the telephone. He was very concerned about his four-year-old son, who was having surgery to correct a cleft palate. The chief's response to Cochran was, "He's a genetic defect. When we come to power, he'll have to be euthanized" (Hochschild, 1994, p. 34).

Cochran reported later that he was stunned by this remark. He had studied Ku Klux Klan and Nazi literature for almost twenty-five years. He did not recognize, nor had he faced until that moment, a sobering fact: The intolerance for difference that he had preached for decades applied to those he loved. When he voiced his concern over this issue, he was given the order to leave the Aryan Nations' property.

The Thawing of a Soul

Eldridge Cleaver, who died in May of 1998, was the author of the startling 1968 book on race and racism, *Soul on Ice*. During the sixties and seventies he was known as a fiery and eloquent voice for the Black Power movement. After the publication of his book, most of which he wrote in prison, he became known as one of the infamous organizers of the Black Panther Party in 1966, along with Huey Newton and Bobby Seale.

In 1968, while serving as Minister of Information for the Black Panthers, Cleaver was involved in a shootout with police in Oakland, California. Wounded in the gun battle, he was arrested. He later jumped bail and fled to Algeria, where he headed the party's so-called international headquarters until there was a major split in the party in the early seventies, with Newton and Seale advocating nonviolence and Cleaver continuing to preach the use of violent methods. Cleaver returned to the United States in 1975. After a long legal battle, he was convicted of assault, placed on probation, and required to do public service.

In *Soul on Ice*, Cleaver spoke with rage of the experiences of African Americans, and with angry disbelief of the oblivious attitudes of most white people regarding their own racism. It is rare to find a line in the book that does not scream with bitterness. And yet, Cleaver closes one of his chapters with these words: "The price of hating other human beings is loving oneself less" (Cleaver, 1968, p. 29).

In the years following his return to the United States, Eldridge Cleaver was not visible as a public figure. He was no longer regarded as a symbol of race pride and race rage. Cleaver's historic identity, however, continued to be that of a figure associated with a separatist philosophy and a militant strategy toward race relations. Given that persona, it is interesting to consider some of the public remarks he made in the early nineties about his youngest child, Riley, who was born with Down syndrome. Cleaver made these statements after he became an activist and advocate for children and adults with disabilities.

In a 1993 speech, Cleaver described his feelings when he learned that his expected son had proven positive for Down syndrome on an amniocentesis test. He spoke candidly of his lack of understanding of the implications of the test, and his insensitivity to the humanity and needs of the child who was to come into his life. He admitted, in fact, that the only thing he did was to follow the lead of his child's mother in accepting and preparing for Riley.

With Riley's birth came the barrage of terms and decisions that often engulf parents of children with disabilities. Cleaver found that the birth of his son coincided with a period when he was questioning himself about his own future. He was no longer a leader of the Black Panther Party, but he did see a role for himself in the civil rights movement in the 1990s. With the birth of a child with Down syndrome, however, Cleaver said,

> I no longer had to wonder what I was going to do, I was doing it. I had my hands full. . . . It was a struggle to understand and comprehend the situation itself, and it was a shock and a struggle to begin to realize that I was involved in a very hostile environment. I began to meet other parents. . . . We began to realize that we were up against the school system, and the legal system, and the medical system. (1993, p. 5)

When Cleaver described his feelings of being "up against" the various social systems of his culture as his son's advocate, his words were reminiscent of the anger he expressed concerning American racism in *Soul on Ice.* And yet, through his struggle to ensure that his son was not the victim of the same kind of prejudice and exclusion that he had raged against decades earlier, Cleaver encountered a new struggle within himself.

Cleaver described a situation with a child he encountered when he took his son Riley to a regional center each day after school. He saw that Riley, who typically had an embrace for everyone as he arrived at the center, always had a special kiss for this one little girl. Cleaver admitted that he was repulsed by the girl because she drooled saliva constantly. Soon the little girl showed that she was happy to see both Riley and his father each day. At first there were just handshakes for Cleaver, then one day she offered him a hug and a kiss.

> She stood up and came at me, and she was salivating, and I felt myself recoil. I looked at her face . . . and I realized that she was reaching out in faith. And I realized that it would be devastating to her if I . . . rejected her . . . that confrontation with myself was really a godsend, and it changed me again, and I embraced the little girl, and I'm so glad that I did that, because at that moment of

resolving that, it gave me an insight into the condition of humanity! (Cleaver, 1993, p. 7)

THE VALUE OF DISABILITY

People with disabilities have the capacity to enrich our personal and social lives. The deficiency and defect models of disability have, however, clouded our ability to see their value. More than a decade ago, Wolf Wolfensberger (1988) identified a number of strengths that people with mental retardation, for example, may bring to their relationships with others. Among these attributes are:

- A natural and positive spontaneity
- A tendency to respond to others generously and warmly
- A tendency to respond honestly to others
- The capacity to call forth gentleness, patience, and tolerance from others
- A tendency to be trusting of others (pp. 63–70)

Many of the disability "stories" that I have told in my writing and in lectures, and many of those that have been told to me, include references to the positive characteristics of people with disabilities. When I reflect on the importance of these children and adults, and their qualities, I find I must say something that I have often lacked the courage to say directly and publicly: A disability can be a valuable human attribute. People with disabilities can be powerful in the humanizing influence they have on others. I am glad that I have had friends with disabilities for most of my life.

In his 1988 book *The Power of the Powerless*, Christopher de Vinck describes the experience of growing up with his brother, Oliver, who was born with multiple and severe disabilities. In his work as an English teacher, de Vinck often told his students about his brother: "One day, during my first year of teaching, I was trying to describe Oliver's lack of response, how he had been spoon-fed every morsel he ever ate, how he never spoke. A boy in the last row raised his hand and said, 'Oh, Mr. de Vinck. You mean he was a vegetable.' . . . Well, I guess you could call him a vegetable. I called him Oliver, my brother. You would have loved him" (de Vinck, 1988, p. 9).

Christopher de Vinck describes Oliver as the weakest human being he ever met. The irony, however, is that he also describes his brother as one of the most powerful human beings he ever knew. When de Vinck assesses the effort and hope that go into teaching and writing and parenting, he thinks of the impact that Oliver had on his life: "Oliver could do absolutely nothing except breathe, sleep, eat and yet he was responsible for action, love, courage and insight. . . . [This] explains to a great degree why I am the type of husband, father, writer and teacher I have become" (de Vinck, 1988, p. 12).

There is most certainly a human ecology of power and compassion. People with disabilities have an important place in that ecological balance. The power of those who have traditionally been considered powerless may be important to our health as human beings and as cultural groups. A person with a disability may temper hateful and prejudicial attitudes. A person with mental retardation may soften a heart that has become hardened. A person with multiple and severe disabilities may have much to teach us about love.

REFERENCES AND FURTHER READINGS

Cleaver, E. (1968). *Soul on ice.* New York: McGraw-Hill.

Cleaver, E. (1993, Fall). Eldridge Cleaver speaks out. *TASH Newsletter, 22,* 4–7.

de Vinck, C. (1988). *The power of the powerless.* New York: Doubleday.

Hochschild, A. (1994, May/June). Changing colors. *Mother Jones,* 27–35.

Rout, K. (1991). *Eldridge Cleaver.* Boston: Twayne.

Wolfensberger, W. (1988). Common assets of mentally retarded people that are not commonly acknowledged. *Mental Retardation, 26,* 64–70.

Part I

My Own Journey

Professors are sometimes accused of leading lives of detachment from the very realities of the world they study and teach about. This accusation is necessarily true in some respects. The only means for truly seeing an intellectual, artistic, or social vista may be to stand at a distance and look at people, events, and objects. Having spent most of my adult life as a college and university professor, I have had the privilege of doing just this.

The work of standing back and observing the changing cultural horizon contrasts sharply, however, with my earlier experiences as a public school teacher, counselor, and Peace Corps volunteer. My present position is also far removed from my intense and challenging work with children and adults with disabilities while I was a high school and college student. In places such as Camp Easter Seal, the Virginia Treatment Center for Children, and the Virginia Home, I learned I could make a direct and positive difference in the lives of others. I also learned that I enjoyed making a difference.

While my wife, Joyce, and I served in the Peace Corps in Jamaica, I discovered that I was pulled to another level of work, assisting people who would in turn help others, thereby amplifying my efforts. My work with the Jamaican Ministry of Education fostered in me a sense of the importance of systemic change. I came to believe that my work in life should somehow involve working with other people to create ripples of positive change.

Living in Jamaica taught me other things as well. I learned much about how little we in the United States understand about the lives of most people in the world that surrounds us. Joyce and I came home having rarely glimpsed the resorts that dominate the American image of the country we had come to love for its sense of pride, purpose, and dignity. We also returned with a deeper sense of the complexity of the social world in which we all live and the challenge of defining one's place in it. Each of the stories in this part of *In Search of Better Angels* is a chapter in my personal journey. These are stories from my childhood, adolescence, and adult life that have molded my views of life, my values, and my work. Each is precious to me and I share them with you, the reader, with the hope that you will find meaning in them as well.

1

Disability and Revelation

Lessons Learned and Flying Squirrels

Like many people in the field of special education, I often ponder what we really mean today when we use the term *learning disabled*. How valid are the concepts that underlie the term, and how well served are children when we describe them as having learning disabilities? In the midst of these ponderings I sometimes remember a boy from my childhood. Most people thought he was not very bright, but he helped me learn lessons that have been deeply meaningful in my life. These were lessons about fish and squirrels and about schools and values.

I first met the boy when I was in the seventh grade in a small rural school. My family had moved during the preceding summer from our home in the city. In my old school, I had been with the same children each year up through the sixth grade. My first few days at the new school were frightening for me. Most of the students in my class seemed older and larger. I was still at an awkward, in-between point in my development. Although puberty had not arrived for me, some of the boys in my seventh grade class were already shaving. Some of the girls also showed clear signs of adolescent development. Suddenly I felt like I was going to school with grown men and women, which was very intimidating. I longed to be back with the other children in my old school in the city.

The boy I remember during my musings on learning disabilities was one of the tallest of the boys in my class. He was big and his looks were imposing, but he was very quiet. In fact, he was shy and the brunt of many jokes. He was rarely able to answer questions from the teacher, and this inability was mocked. He was often unable to finish seatwork or chalkboard problems, and this became fodder for constant teasing. Even though he was larger than most of the other boys, he took their kidding and even their ridicule without retaliating. He was an easy target for harsh jokes about his appearance. He was large, but everyone called him Tiny. Even though this was a spoof on his size, his real name was so unusual that it was also used as a source of ridicule. And so he preferred to be called Tiny.

I thought Tiny was just as strange as the others thought he was. Although in this little rural school nobody had great wealth, Tiny's clothing clearly showed signs of being handed down for several more recyclings than most. The lunches he brought to school were obviously made from whatever had been left from his family's supper the night before. Sometimes he brought stale biscuits and cold cooked vegetables. This was quite different from the standard fare of peanut butter sandwiches and fruit that most of us brought from home. Tiny was always clean and neat, but it was obvious to all that his family was poor.

It was not only his poverty that made him appear strange to the other seventh graders, but also the fact that he was a loner. He usually rode on the school bus in a seat by himself. He rarely spoke to anyone, and he often gave only one-word responses when he was asked questions. Tiny had younger sisters. If he were seen talking with anyone at school, it would be with them. The only sign of assertiveness that I ever saw in him was in his protectiveness of his sisters. I do not recall anything specific about his care of them, but I know that people understood that although he would not respond to their attacks on him, he would not let his sisters be hurt.

After the first couple of months of school, however, I got to know Tiny in a different light. In fact, we became friends. It happened, at least partially, because I had become a loner at the new school myself. I was the only new student in the seventh grade and, as I have said, I had not yet hit that spurt of growth that would propel me into adolescence. I lacked confidence in myself and was still too childlike to fit in very well with most of my new classmates.

After school each day I spent time alone. One afternoon I explored a cornfield that was brown and dry with the remains of an earlier harvest. I had overheard some of the other kids say that somewhere beyond the field was a pond. I discovered the pond that sunny November day but, more important, I found a friend. As I climbed over the fence that surrounded the pond I saw Tiny. He was fishing. He watched me climb awkwardly over the barbed wire and nodded. We were both embarrassed at having stumbled onto each other, but there was no way to avoid a conversation. I'm not sure who spoke first, but I think it must have been me. Even though I had become a loner in my new environment, of the two of us, Tiny was definitely the more private person.

That afternoon I learned how to fish for what Tiny called sunfish. In telling me about them, he talked more than I had ever heard him talk. He told me with enthusiasm, for example, that some people called sunfish either panfish or crappies. Crappie, panfish, or sunfish—the pond was full of them! So full, apparently, that there was ferocious competition among them for food. We fished using balls of sandwich bread on hooks with four prongs, and we sometimes caught two fish on the same line. The fish seemed to leap for the bait as soon as it hit the water. When we ran out of bread, Tiny showed me how to pull the hook through the water and snag the hungry fish with bare metal. He had a bucket of water that we put the fish into to keep them alive. Periodically he would check the bucket and pick out the smaller fish that had not been injured too badly by the hooks and return them to the pond. After all of our fishing was done, Tiny strung the fish that he wanted to take home on a long piece of cord. He strung a share for me.

Tiny then led me on a shortcut through the cornfield, over the railroad tracks that bordered it, and up a path that led to the back of his house. His house was very modest and covered with asphalt-shingled siding. He invited me into the kitchen, which was off the back porch. His sisters were busy helping their mother with supper. They were surprised and embarrassed to have me suddenly appear in their home. Tiny's mother, however, was delighted to see us and soon made everyone feel more comfortable. She had a bright smile and gentle manner. I liked her immediately. She was glad to have the fish and quickly had the girls cleaning them for cooking.

We talked for a little while about school, the pond, and the fish. And then I left, walking the short distance to my own home, feeling glad that I had come to know Tiny. I looked forward to seeing him again.

Although we barely spoke at school, I spent lots of afternoons fishing with Tiny. One day in January we went sliding on the frozen pond and played ice hockey with dead oak branches and a flat rock. Although most of the pond was frozen thick, I broke through near the bank. Both of my legs went into the icy water up to the knees. Tiny helped me get out, and he built a fire to warm my feet and to dry my shoes and jeans. He always seemed to know how to take care of things like that. Tiny, who was wise and mature beyond his years in many ways, liked helping people when given the chance.

The next fall we went to the eighth grade together at the high school. We had continued our friendship during the summer and worked together to earn spending money. I was accustomed to making money by mowing lawns, delivering newspapers, and working at a golf course. Tiny involved me in *real* work. We loaded pulpwood, which were long pine logs, onto a railroad flatcar. This was the most exhausting, dirtiest, and discouraging work that I had ever tried. It rivals any demanding physical work I have done since. The more wood we loaded on the flatcar, the bigger the stack of logs on the siding seemed to grow. Several times a day a truck would arrive from the cutting site on a nearby mountain with even more wood! The logs were thrown from the truck in a haphazard fashion that looked a lot easier than the lifting we were doing to get them up onto and in place on the flatcar. I came close to crying at times. I was tired, scratched, and bleeding from the pinebark, and I wished that I could somehow escape the commitment to finish the job. In reality, Tiny did more than his share of the work. I took frequent and long breaks. He never complained and kept working while I rested, yet he shared with me equally the money we were paid when the job was over. The whole experience was a great motivational lesson for me. It convinced me of the wisdom of staying in school and "getting an education."

Things did not go well for Tiny during our first year at high school. We had no classes together, but I knew that he was not happy. Socially, he continued to be a loner, and at the high school he was teased by an even larger number of students. Again, he never retaliated. He suffered the insults about his size, his shyness, and his poor school performance in silence. I don't remember ever coming to his defense. I'm sure I lacked the maturity and insight to do so.

Our friendship after school and on weekends continued. I enjoyed his company, and he always seemed happy to see me. We went fishing, took hikes, and once made a dam in the creek that ran at the foot of the hill below his house. We put some of the smaller fish that we caught in the pond into the pooled water. We shared good times, but we never talked about school.

After our first year in high school, I saw even less of Tiny. When we started classes the next September, he was still classified as an eighth grader and his schedule was completely different from mine. The next year he didn't return to school. It turned out that Tiny had failed some grades in elementary school and was actually a couple of years older than me. He was old enough to drop out of high school.

The next time I talked with Tiny, he gave me a very short answer to my question about school. "I'm just a slow learner, that's what they said. I can't make it in school anymore and I have to find something else to do now." He told me this as we were exploring in the woods just beyond the pond. A year earlier he had shown me how to harvest mistletoe there. His technique was based on his excellent aim with a 22-caliber rifle. He lay on his back and shot the mistletoe out of the oak branches where it grew in the large and damp tree joints. He explained to me that his mother sent him to the woods every year around that time to shoot mistletoe. She decorated the mistletoe with ribbons and sold them to neighbors for Christmas trimmings. Tiny was a good marksman. He showed me that it took good aim to knock out only part of the plant, which he told me was what he was trying to do because if the whole plant was blown out of the tree there would be no new growth for next year.

This time we were walking in the woods behind the pond to see something special that he had found. Under a big oak, he pulled back a rustling cover of dry leaves to reveal a cardboard box. Inside the box were shredded rags swaddling a baby squirrel. It was special, he explained—it was a flying squirrel. Earlier in the day he had seen it helpless and trembling under the tree. Tiny knew flying squirrels forage for food at night. He planned to return the baby to the nest that night while the mother was hunting. He told me I could help.

That night, I held a flashlight as Tiny scaled the tree with the baby squirrel in a cloth bag he had tied to his belt loop. He gently put the baby in the nest and then climbed back down the tree. As far as I know, the reunion was a success. On our walk back to his house, I asked Tiny how he knew so much about flying squirrels. He explained that he had learned it all from what he called his "books." When I asked what books he was talking about, he told me that he had an old set of encyclopedias that he read at night. It was a set that his mother had found for him. I have no idea what the circumstances were of her acquiring them, but he showed them to me with great pride. They were dated volumes, old and mildewed, but they were readable and he stored them carefully in a crate under his bed.

I was amazed! The boy who had dropped out of school and thought he was slow was a researcher. When I asked about this seeming contradiction, Tiny told me that he could "read fine" when he had enough time and when he wasn't going to be taking a test. He liked to read and he loved to learn, but he just couldn't do it the way it was done in school.

Education was defined narrowly during my years in school. Learning was to be done the standard way or not at all. During the years that I knew Tiny, I didn't know anything about individual learning needs or what would come to be known as learning disabilities. I did know, however, that something was terribly wrong when the rescuer of flying squirrels and an expert on their habits and habitat thought that he was too slow, too different, to be in school.

The rescue of the baby flying squirrel was the last adventure that Tiny and I shared. Events took us in different directions and I don't recall having had another conversation with him. I am sure that we must have seen each other after that, but I just don't remember it.

When I first thought of writing down my memories of Tiny, I began to wonder if I had simply forgotten that he eventually came back to school. I pulled out old yearbooks and searched for his face in the classes of each of my high school years. He wasn't there. I also searched my memory for any recollection of him during those years. I could remember nothing.

On a recent trip to my hometown I asked some old friends about Tiny. I found that I wasn't experiencing memory lapses as I had feared. Tiny never returned to school. For a while he found odd jobs that allowed him to help his mother and sisters. Finally he found a way to help them even more—he joined the army. My friends say that Tiny took care of his mother and sisters by sending money home for them.

A disturbing discovery came from my inquiries: Like many other boys of my generation who left school, and who joined or were drafted into the military, Tiny died in Vietnam. Without the options of educational deferments or the other opportunities that might have been available to him if he had more education, Tiny was sent to the front lines of the conflict. I know nothing of the circumstances of his death, but I have imagined that he died in a jungle. In my imaginings, I have hoped that he had a chance to see and be close to jungle animals before he was killed. Maybe he rescued a few. Maybe if he had returned from the jungle he would have looked them up in his "books."

If Tiny had lived in a time and place that defined ability and courage more broadly than the schools of our youth did, he might have been seen as a bright and brave young man with great potential for learning. Instead, he died serving a system that viewed him, and taught him to view himself, as slow and as a dropout. I am grateful that I had the opportunity to know him as something more. I trust that our society and our schools have become and are becoming even more open, inclusive, and compassionate. I hope that there is a place for those with Tiny's talents in our schools today. I trust that he would have been truly helped by the opportunities available now. I hope that he would have been helped, rather than further handicapped, by being recognized as having a learning disability. I hope that he would have had the opportunity to help other people the way that he helped me.

Flying squirrels live in the hollows of trees. They hunt for food at night. They usually have babies twice each year. They glide from the highest branches, swoop low, and then soar higher again. Thanks for the lesson, Tiny.

2

Learning to Love,
Loving to Learn

Mike and the Clown Faces

The first year in the classroom is memorable for most teachers. For some new educators, it can be a year of such painful memories in the making that a career has ended before June. For others, it is a year that provides war stories and lessons in survival from which they build a lifetime of continued learning.

Frankly, my first year of teaching came as the result of avoidance. I was in graduate school, draft deferments for graduate students had ended, and I was seeking a way of serving other than through the military. In other words, and again quite frankly, I did not want to be drafted. I had been asked to work in a rehabilitation facility. The director wrote a letter on my behalf, but my draft board would not grant a deferment on that basis. I made a personal appearance to appeal this decision. The appeal was unsuccessful, but the attorney who was appointed to represent me called me aside after the hearing and suggested that I could be deferred for work with children with disabilities, that is, if I could find a special education teaching job. Deferments were still being granted for teachers in critical need areas, and special education was one of those areas. I immediately began my search for a position.

My first day of seeking a teaching job was illusively successful. I went to the school system's personnel office and was greeted with enthusiasm. The receptionist glanced at the short application I filled out. It indicated that I was interested in a special education position. She asked that I wait for just a moment. When she returned, she told me that the Director of Personnel would like to talk with me right away. Within twenty minutes he had offered me a job and was urging me to sign a contract before leaving his office. There was an opening for a teacher of children with "emotional problems," and he was convinced that I was just the right person for the position. I asked to have a little more time to think about it. He agreed and said that I could come back the next day with my decision. I will admit that I left his office with the youthful confidence that I was a pretty impressive candidate. I had been offered a job on the spot! I had a lot to learn.

The next day I accepted the position. I completed all the necessary paperwork and was told when and where to report before the opening of school. I learned that my class was made up of all boys. They varied in age, and the only thing they had in common was the label "serious emotional disturbance." In fact, once I had signed the contract, the Director of Personnel started calling these boys the "dead-end kids." They had all been expelled from their schools. Most of them had been in trouble with the law, and many of them had been given up by their families to foster care. I would be teaching them in a "special education center," which turned out to be an old house with four other classes of "dead-end kids."

During the teacher workdays, before the children came to school, it became obvious to me why the Director of Personnel had greeted me with such enthusiasm and offered me this job on the spot. The veteran teachers of the "dead-end kids" bombarded me with horror stories. They informed me that the class I was to teach had been through two teachers before Christmas the year before. My qualifications for the job, it became obvious, were my naïveté and the fact that I was male and over six feet tall. I suppose the assumption was that I might have a better chance of controlling these children because I was likely to be larger than most of them. This, of course, was a bad assumption. These were children who were, for the most part, unintimidated by size, age, or gender. They had become experts at finding ways of winning power struggles of all kinds.

The first day of school came too quickly for me. I knew that I was not prepared to deal with the boys who had been described to me. Even though there were to be only eight of them, and I had a full-time teaching assistant, I knew that I was unprepared to meet the educational needs of the students. I had begun to doubt my ability to survive as their teacher. My background as a psychology major in college, who had done graduate work in clinical psychology, was helpful to me as I read the case histories of the boys. Nevertheless, I had no idea of where to begin as their teacher. The records showed that they ranged in age from seven to fifteen. There were both nonreaders and excellent readers in the group, and their levels of skill did not necessarily correspond to their ages. Some of the older boys had weaker academic skills than the younger ones.

I tried to prepare for them as best as I could. My few teacher workdays before the opening of school, however, were not enough to allow me to make up for my lack of training. It was not enough time for me to be ready to teach the academic skills that the boys needed to develop. It was not enough time to devise a strategy for helping them develop the sense of self and the social skills that they would need to have a chance to be something other than "dead-end kids." I used the time I had to do what I could to make the environment of the classroom (actually two converted bedrooms) as orderly and attractive as possible.

I cleaned the desks and arranged the rest of the furniture in the larger of the two rooms into what I thought was a pleasant configuration. I moved some of the extra desks and what appeared to be leftover supplies into the room next door. The director of the center had told me that I could use the room as I saw fit. It was as large as my classroom and was the perfect place for stashing everything I wanted to get out of the way. I envisioned, even then, that it might also become a place for "cooling down," either for the boys or for myself.

I had excellent help in getting the room ready. In fact, my most encouraging discovery after reporting for work was that my teaching assistant, Miss Boyer, was a person of calm confidence. She had been an art major in the college from which she'd recently graduated. Although she shared my inexperience and lack of training as a teacher, she was filled with optimism about what we would be able to accomplish with the children we were about to meet. She had lots of ideas for decorating the room for the opening of school and for ways that we could make each boy's desk personally welcoming. Soon we had filled the walls with her creations and stocked each boy's desk with paper and other supplies. Each desk had a laminated nameplate across the front. After a week of preparation and planning, my teaching assistant and I were as prepared as possible to meet our students.

On Monday morning, the first boy to arrive was Mike. He was very early. His mother brought him on her way to work and dropped him off about twenty minutes before any of the other children arrived. This pattern persisted throughout the school year. What also persisted was Mike's calling me "Smith." Although we introduced ourselves to Mike as Mr. Smith and Miss Boyer, I was "Smith" for the rest of the year not only to Mike but to the other boys, who soon picked up on this name for me. Miss Boyer was referred to by her complete name.

As soon as Mike entered the room, the atmosphere changed. Mike was in constant motion and seemed to create energy even in inanimate objects. Everything he touched, and that seemed to be everything, was energized. I directed Mike to his desk and showed him the supplies we had placed there for him. He immediately asked if he could draw a picture on one of the large pieces of drawing paper.

The picture that Mike drew was of a clown. He drew it quickly and mechanically. It appeared that Mike had drawn this picture before. The clown face consisted of a large circle with semicircles for ears, smaller circles for eyes, a round nose, and a crescent mouth. A bowler hat with a broad brim topped it.

When Mike finished the clown, he asked if he could use another piece of paper from his desk. He changed the color of the marker he used, but the image was the same. He drew the clown again in exactly the same sequence of parts. First he drew the round head, then the ears, then the eyes, nose, and mouth. He finished with the bowler hat and immediately asked to use yet another piece of paper.

Before the other boys arrived, Mike had produced a stack of clown faces that he placed in a neat pile on his desk. As the other students came in, and Miss Boyer and I were greeting them, Mike requested and was given more drawing paper. He produced even more clown faces.

The next few weeks were some of the most difficult of my life. I came home at the end of each day with an amalgam of negative feelings. The boys exhausted me; I felt absolutely ineffectual as their teacher, and I disliked them and myself. I doubted that I could make it to Thanksgiving, and Christmas, I was certain, was an impossible goal.

The boys became increasingly disruptive and aggressive as the weeks went by. The language that they used was truly creative in its vulgarity. The academic progress that we could make with them was practically nil. Each boy had developed his own way of avoiding the failure that he had come to associate with schoolwork. Some of the boys would explode with anger when they were unable to do their work. Others would become clowns in an attempt to show that they really didn't care if they couldn't do the work. Mike simply drew his clowns. Regardless of the task I gave him or the material I put before him, he ended up drawing the same clown face using exactly the same sequence of movements with his marker. It never varied. I came to understand that it was the one thing he knew he could do well, and he drew the face as a comforting compulsion to avoid the pain of not being able to read, write, or do math.

I reached a point of absolute desperation in my work with the boys, and I finally sought help. I literally put myself in the doorway of a professor's office at the university where I had previously studied, pleading for assistance. He was a professor of special education, and one of my former psychology professors had recommended him as a possible source of ideas for bringing some order and rationality to what I was doing as a teacher. This man allowed me in, listened to my plight, and, most important, gave me several simple guidelines to think about. He also gave me a book that proved to be very helpful.

The pieces of advice were these: First, in all academic subject areas, take each student back to the point where he can show mastery of a skill. Sometimes this meant taking an older student back to letter or number recognition before proceeding with any further reading or math instruction at all. This, of course, had to be accomplished in a way that allowed the student to preserve his dignity; he could not feel that you were giving him "baby work." Second, proceed with instruction in small steps. Small enough, in fact, that you can be sure that the student will be successful. Students who have been hurt by failure must come to trust that you will not give them work that they can't do. They must know that you are a teacher who will not let them fail. Third, you must make their successes dramatically obvious to them. Their success must be concretely and vividly displayed to them. Their victories must be immediately and enthusiastically acknowledged.

The book that the professor gave me helped me to rethink the use of the space we had. As a result of reading it, Miss Boyer and I moved all of the desks into the room that we had been using for storage and placed them along the walls. We then built cardboard partitions between the desks to give the boys "offices" for doing the work that we had individualized for them. In their offices, the boys did the reading, language arts, and math that most of them had experienced failure with previously. In the privacy of their offices, however, Miss Boyer and I were able to follow the professor's advice. We took each boy back to the level where success was a certainty, and we moved ahead in increments that also ensured success. The work and office schedule of each boy was personalized and private. There was no stigma of "baby work" associated with what was done in the offices. Miss Boyer and I moved from office to office as "consultants," helping each boy individually.

Our larger classroom became a group activity area. We started and ended each day there as a class. We also used it for social studies, art, and other activities that the boys could share regardless of their level of academic ability. We posted schedules in this room daily so that when the boys arrived in the morning each could check for any variations in his daily routine. There were few variations, but the boys liked the certainty of their posted schedules.

We also began a simple token economy system that allowed the boys to earn extra free time, pencils, drawing paper, and markers through the points they earned for focused work time in their offices and the successful completion of assignments. In addition, we made sure that we used traditional ways of recognizing good work. Papers were graded immediately upon completion and were marked with number grades, letter grades, and comments.

Mike responded very well to our new system of rewards. At first, as might be expected, he used the points he earned to buy drawing paper and markers, which he then used for the production of lots of clown faces. At least, however, he was now doing his work in order to have the satisfaction and comfort of the familiar drawings. After a while, however, Miss Boyer and I noticed that Mike's interest in paper and markers was diminishing. We also noticed that he was producing far fewer of the clown drawings that he had taken home earlier in the year in stacks. He seemed instead to be more interested in taking home the math and reading papers that we carefully graded in bold markers with "100, A, Good Work." We shared Mike's gratification in having these papers now going home with him in stacks.

I don't mean to give the impression that suddenly everything was perfect in our class. There were still arguments and blowups. There were still harsh expressions of frustration. Yet as Miss Boyer and I became better organized in our learning environment and schedules, and as the boys experienced greater success academically, their behavior improved. They became children who were more pleasant to be with. They had more positive attitudes toward themselves and about their abilities to learn. Miss Boyer and I also felt a change in the ways the boys behaved toward us. They were clearly happy to see us each morning, and even the toughest boys showed signs of affection for us on occasion.

One December morning, I gave the boys some exciting news. The afternoon before, I had been told as I was leaving school that a civic group would be coming the next morning to give a party for the children. We would gather in the lunchroom (a converted area in the basement of the building) at 10:30 for ice cream, candy, and gifts. When we gathered for our morning group meeting, I told the boys about the party. Most were excited about the news. Mike, however, protested immediately that he couldn't go to the party. When I asked why, he said, "Smith, you know I have math to do at 10:30. I will be in my office then." When I explained that today was special and that we were changing the usual morning schedule, he protested even more loudly, "Smith, I'm not going to the damn party till I finish my math."

At 10:30 Miss Boyer took the other boys to the party. Mike stayed in his office and I brought him his math assignment, which he worked on diligently for fifteen minutes. When he was finished, I congratulated him and suggested that we join the others at the party. He agreed, but said, "Smith, you forgot something." I looked down and realized that he was waiting for me to grade his work. I reviewed it and marked it "100, A, Good Work." Mike smiled, filed his work away, and said, "Now, Smith, we can go to that party."

On our way down the hall, Mike explained why following his schedule was so important to him. "Smith," he said more openly than I had ever heard him speak before, "My mama loves the papers I bring home. She hugs me and tells me I'm getting smarter all the time. She saves my papers. She says you and Miss Boyer are good teachers. I think so, too. My uncle teaches good, too. He taught me how to draw clowns, but I like math better now."

Learning to love, loving to learn. I think often of Mike and the others. I am grateful for all that I learned from them on my journey to becoming a teacher. I'm glad they helped me take the first few steps.

3

Inclusion, Exclusion, and Other Matters of the Heart

The Story of Nan

My years in elementary school in Roanoke, Virginia, were markedly without children who were really different in any significant way from our next-door-neighbor norms. There were no children of African American heritage, no children who spoke a different native tongue, and no children with disabilities. School in the world of my community was for those children who met some unarticulated but well-understood standard of normality.

There were, of course, the Wilk children, who came to school, even in the frost of fall, without shoes; that they came from a poor family was self-evident. Everyone knew that their ragged clothes and body odor made them different. They got low grades and were not invited to birthday parties. Even with their blond hair and agile bodies, they were eyed with pity and humor because of the low step on the elementary school hierarchy that they occupied. I remember Daniel, the oldest of the many Wilks in our school. He was my classmate for several years. Daniel was good at kickball, even with his bare, calloused feet; but I cringed when his turn came to read in Mrs. Weaver's third-grade class. Yet I also giggled with the others at his mistakes and hesitations. Eventually Daniel learned to laugh at himself—not a participatory, good-humored laugh, as I now understand, but a laugh of defense, of self-protection.

One day, the Wilk children came to school with patches of shaved scalp and purple medicine glistening on their heads. Ringworm. Somehow, we all knew that this was just more evidence that the Wilks were dirty, defective, and different.

One day the Wilk kids were gone. Mrs. Ramble, the fourth-grade teacher who was known for expressing her opinions candidly, explained that those Wilk children have moved back to the sticks, where they belong. She explained to us that the Wilk children did not belong in school in the first place: School is for children who can learn—you can't teach trash.

My only other experience with diversity in those elementary school years involved a little girl I will call Nan. She was what might have been called an honorary member of my classes for several years. Nan did not come to our classroom except on special occasions. She came to the Christmas party on the last day of school before the holiday break and received her cookies and candy canes. At the Valentine's Day party, she came to collect the brown paper bag full of the cards we had all been instructed to bring her. At school assemblies, Nan was rolled into the cafetorium in her wheelchair after the lights were lowered.

Nan had no arms, and her legs were short, one more so than the other. She looked much like those children who, a few years later, came to be known as thalidomide babies. I don't think I wondered much about the reason for her disability, or anything else about her, in my narrow grasp of the human condition at the time. All that I remember is thinking of her as the curious crippled girl who came to school on holidays. I don't think I ever got close to her; I'm sure that I never spoke with her.

A few years passed, my family moved from the city to the country, and I found myself focused on the importance of being a teenager. Shortly after my sixteenth birthday, I decided that I was a man. Recognizing my maturity, and after several confrontations with my parents over their failure to realize it, I made a resolution. I had to find a way to get away from home during the coming summer vacation from school. I made several bold but (I thought) reasonable propositions to my parents. I would travel with a couple of older guys who were graduating and were going to be selling magazines in North Carolina and South Carolina. No? Well, I could spend the summer picking fruit with the crews that went from orchard to orchard in the region. I would never really be that far from home. No! Misery.

Finally, my big break came. One day, while listening to the best rock and roll station in the Star City of the South, I heard an announcement that would change my life. Just how much, I didn't realize at the time. A summer camp was looking for junior counselors. No experience was necessary, and you only had to be sixteen years old to apply. I wrote down the number, called, and asked that an application be sent to me.

I hardly noticed that it was to Camp Easter Seal that I was sending my employment application. I suppose that I had some vague notion that it was crippled kids who attended the camp. The important thing, however, was that this was my chance to get away from home for the summer. It worked. In early June I was on the road to adventure with the opportunity to be the independent adult I was convinced I could be.

The first few days at Camp Easter Seal were glorious. There were lots of others like me there, both male and female. There were even some college women. The summer held great promise.

On the second day of orientation for new counselors, we went to various activity areas to see what the children would be doing, and how we were to assist them. After visiting the pool for a lecture from the lifeguard, we toured the nature study cabin, learned the joys of relay racing from the director of athletics, and learned the camp song from the music coordinator. Our final stop was arts and crafts.

We were met at the door by the very enthusiastic director of the program. She was bright, beautiful, and excited about making popsicle-stick baskets and mosaic-tile ashtrays with the kids. She was one of the college women. I was immediately dedicated to doing all that I could to promote the arts that summer.

I was so occupied that I did not notice the young woman sitting on the table at the back of the room until the director introduced her as the assistant director of arts and crafts. She had no arms, her legs were very short, and she was mixing tempera paint with a tongue depressor that she held between her toes. Her smile was radiant. It was Nan, who had been coming to the camp since she was ten. After six years as a camper, she had been hired as a staff member. I immediately recognized her, but embarrassment held me back from mentioning to her that we had met before. In a real sense, of course, we had not. It was weeks later that I finally told her that we had been classmates at Morningside Elementary.

Through the summer, I came to know Nan as a talented and captivating person. She had learned to use her feet for most of the things that normal people use hands to do—and more. She typed, played an electric piano, and was learning guitar. The counselors and the children were drawn to her. She was a great talker, a sensitive listener, and a marvelous laugher. We talked about politics and religion and philosophy as we knew them at that time in our adolescent lives. We explored the large and general issues of life and became comfortable in sharing the personal fears and hopes that we each harbored. We were remarkably similar. By the end of the summer, I no longer thought of Nan as "the little crippled girl" who had come to school to pick up her Christmas candy and valentines. She had become a person to me, and somehow her disabilities had faded from my perception of her. My understanding of people and vision of life were transformed.

My experience of Nan was an important part of the change that took place in me that summer, but there were other factors that also affected me.

I came to the camp as an exercise in what I perceived to be manhood. Through my work that summer with children with mental retardation, physical disabilities, and speech impairments, I learned lessons in humility, compassion, and caring. I did, in fact, take my first true steps toward adulthood. Work for me up to that time had meant delivering newspapers, mowing lawns, and carrying golf clubs. I learned that work could mean doing something that was critical to the growth of another human being. Things were never quite the same for me again.

At the end of the summer, I returned to my family and another year of high school. It was difficult to explain to my friends what my summer had been about. In fact, it was impossible.

For the next two years, the focus of much of my attention was Camp Easter Seal. Oh, I had my share of high school revelries, perhaps more than my share. Even so, I did manage to devote enough time to my studies to graduate. My memory of that period, however, is that the most important thing for me was being at Camp Easter Seal or thinking of being there.

Each summer, a core group of "regulars" returned to the camp staff. Nan and I were "regulars." We grew in the responsibilities we assumed and in our closeness with each other. Nan was central to the camp. She provided us with inspiration through her optimism and courage. Most important to me, she was a reliable friend. It was easy, and common, to forget that Nan was "missing" anything. In fact, she was not—she had more of most of the truly important human qualities than I did. I readily acknowledged that Nan had much to teach others about being human.

One day toward the end of my third summer at the camp, Nan asked me if we could talk after lunch while the campers were having rest time. We met under a large shade tree outside the dining hall. Nan had been having difficulty making a decision about and working out arrangements for going to college in the fall. She had finally decided on the same school where I would be going and wanted to talk with me about it. I told her how happy I was with her decision. It would really be nice seeing her at college. She knew, however, that there were going to be problems. Some of the buildings had long flights of steps at the entrances. She was also sure that some of her classes would be in second-floor rooms. Getting around in her wheelchair would not be easy. I was quick to reassure her that things would work out, with no major difficulties. I was certain we could arrange classes so that I could help her with any barriers that might exist. Things were going to be fine . . . and being at college with Nan would be a little like being at camp. How neat!

Things did work amazingly well the first week of college. As it turned out, another friend and longtime neighbor of Nan's was also there. Through minimal adjustments, our schedules allowed all of us to get to classes on time and with no trouble. One of us would meet Nan at the steps outside a classroom building, carry her up, go back for her wheelchair, and repeat the procedure at inside stairs if necessary. Nan waited outside her classrooms for the trip down the stairs after the bell. Often the way was crowded with other students, but most were courteous and made sure we had ample room.

Going to college was a great social adventure for me, perhaps in my mind initially more of a social than an academic event. I had purchased my clothing carefully. I wanted to "look college." I had visions of the new girls I would meet, the guys I would be hanging around with, and the parties I would be invited to. I didn't feel the need to be a "Big Man on Campus," but I wanted to be a solidly "cool guy."

Sometimes, as I was carrying Nan or her wheelchair to a class, however, I felt people were staring. It bothered me. I now understand how I could have been troubled by those stares. My difficulty in comprehending their meaning at that time, however, was to have a profound influence on the course of my life.

Camp Easter Seal had been a special place. I am sure that I was not aware while I was there of the many ways it was different from the "real world." The camp was an isolated culture unto itself. Disabilities had a way of disappearing from our perception of people there. As I have said, Nan became, in that environment, a person who was interesting and fun to be with. The fact that she lacked arms, that she did manual things with her feet, became unimportant. But I had known Nan only in that separated, caring, understanding place.

Suddenly I found myself challenged in a very fundamental and disturbing way. Now that I can look back on it, I suppose that during my three summers at Camp Easter Seal I felt that I had overcome the prejudices and misunderstandings of "handicapism." I think I was convinced that I had become a genuine advocate for people with disabilities.

What I now had to admit was that I was embarrassed being seen carrying Nan up and down the steps between classes. I knew that other people at the college didn't understand. Their stares convinced me that I was becoming associated with her disability. They didn't understand about Nan; they wouldn't understand our relationship; I would be stigmatized. What would happen to my college social life?

I detested myself. How shallow I must be. What I had thought was conviction was only convenience: It had been so easy to talk and act as an advocate for people with disabilities in the seclusion and safety, and segregation, of the camp. Now with the slightest test of my beliefs, I was selling out, at least emotionally.

Just as I was about convinced that my social life was headed for the rocks, there was a glimmer of hope. I was invited to the party of the fall season. It was what we called a "cabin party," music and dancing in a rustic and romantic venue. The invitation came from a socially prominent source. All the really "neat" people would be there. Wonderful! What an opportunity to meet the key people on campus. Maybe I would even have a chance to make them understand why I was regularly seen carrying an armless girl.

I arrived at the Friday night event fashionably late and in my best madras shirt. As I entered the large, open room, I looked around for familiar faces. Seeing none, I headed for the refreshments. Filling a milk shake cup with a beverage, I glanced to the corners, again in hopes of finding someone I knew. Most of the people there, however, were standing with their backs to me at the far end of the room. I walked in that direction. When I got close enough, I tried to subtly peek over a shoulder to see what the center of attention was. It was Nan! She was sipping her drink through a straw and telling jokes.

That night, through Nan, I met many people. They were all impressed that I knew her so well. That night, also, Nan unknowingly taught me a lesson that has lasted: Beliefs and commitments, genuine beliefs and commitments, must be public and primary. The lesson I learned from Nan has been a thread connecting the discrete events of my personal life and my career.

At the end of the year, I transferred to another college. Over the next couple of years, I saw Nan very infrequently. Eventually we lost touch with each other altogether. For some years, I had news of her life through mutual friends. She finished college, did graduate work in counseling, and took a position providing rehabilitation services to disabled veterans. I can't think of anyone who could have been a more compassionate and insightful counselor for veterans, particularly those who returned from Vietnam with wounds to body and mind.

A delightful story that was passed along to me about Nan was that a group of prisoners at the state penitentiary heard about her life and work and wanted to do something special for her. It seems that one of them found out that the one thing she most wanted, but had been unable to do, was to drive. Her independence was limited in that sense. Apparently, these men organized a fund-raising campaign, had a van modified for her, and arranged for special driving instruction. With total foot control and a hydraulic lift for getting into the van, she was set free on the highways. The story goes that her only difficulty has been the speeding tickets she's received on the interstate highways.

I have often talked of Nan to my students. As I relate her story and others from my personal experience, I am reminded of the reality of exclusion—and the promise of inclusion—in the lives of people with disabilities. This, in turn, has led me to reflect on and examine the central role of integration, of an ethic of inclusiveness, in the field of education. Children with disabilities deserve to be valued and fully included in the lives of our schools. Adults with disabilities need to be seen not as people who are "missing" something, who are incomplete or defective, but as people whose presence we welcome. I also recognize that although legislation and litigation can grant rights and provide programs, true inclusion is a matter of the heart. It will happen when our society has a change of heart about people with disabilities. I think the change has begun, and I am gratified to see it occurring. I am also thankful for Nan, the transformation she brought to my life, and the change of heart she gave me.

Nan and I found each other again during a Thanksgiving holiday a few years ago. I had corresponded with her two years earlier after visiting Camp Easter Seal and inquiring about her there. I had also sent her a copy of the story that I had shared with so many of my students. I was relieved that she liked it!

Nan's real name, which she gave me permission to use, is Norma Milam Garrett. She has been married since 1981 to a wonderful man who obviously loves her dearly. She helped in the raising of his two children from a previous marriage. Norma is now a grandmother. She continues to be a radiant and positive person. I continue to feel fortunate to know her.

4

Disabling Prejudice

Aunt Celie and the Marble Cake

Race issues continue to create dilemmas for our society and for our schools. At times it seems that racism and racial conflict have increased rather than decreased in recent decades. As evidenced by the publication of *The Bell Curve* (1994), arguments for racial differences in intellect and other human attributes continue to be presented and enveloped in the mantle of science. I offer here a few recollections and reflections regarding race. They are given in a spirit of concern and hope. They are intended as appeals for the dignity and respect for all people that must characterize American education if it is to achieve its potential.

One of the most vivid memories I have from my childhood is of a trip to Alabama when I was seven. The trip was a visit with my mother's family in Montgomery. It was my second rail pilgrimage from Virginia to Alabama. The first was when my brother Carl was an infant and I was four. I have no memory at all of that visit. The second time, probably because of their vivid recollection of having traveled with me as a four-year-old, my parents decided to leave Carl, who was now that age, at home with relatives. I remember, and relish even now, the excitement of sleeping in the Pullman car and eating in the dining car. Even more exciting was having the conductor acknowledge our special status. We were traveling on a free pass because my father worked as a machinist in the Norfolk and Western Railway Shops. I even had a chance to ride with the engineer for a few precious minutes.

CELIE

I also clearly remember changing trains in Birmingham, the colossus of the passenger station there, and riding in a new coach on the last leg of the trip into Montgomery. A vendor passed through the car selling sandwiches and snacks from a large metal box. The image of the cardboard cone of shelled peanuts my mother bought and shared has remained with me now for more than five decades.

Arriving in Montgomery on the hot summer night was a sleepy blur for me as a seven-year-old. I remember only that my Uncle Ray picked us up in a big black boat of a car. We made a quick stop at my grandmother's house. It was late, and we soon went on to Uncle Ray's house for something to eat and to go to bed.

The next morning was devoted to a real visit with my grandmother and a stop at the firehouse where my uncle worked. Wearing his fireman's hat, ringing the bell on the hook and ladder truck, and blowing the siren for just a second—these are the sorts of things that childhood memories are supposed to be made of. That afternoon, however, was to grant me another kind of memory, a memory that would echo through the rest of my life.

My mother had often talked with me about a woman she called Aunt Celie. I knew that Celie was an African American woman who had been very kind to my mother when she was a little girl. I had heard descriptions many times of how Aunt Celie brushed my mother's hair and told her stories of her own childhood. My mother had told me that Celie was a slave when she was a very young child. Somehow, however, this had made no particular impression on me and did not find a special place in my mind.

That afternoon in Montgomery, we went to Aunt Celie's home. My perceptions of her, of my mother, and of human relationships were changed profoundly as a result of that visit. When we drove up to Aunt Celie's house in Uncle Ray's Buick, my mother could not wait to get out of the car. Her feet were barely on the sidewalk when she was met by squeals of laughter and delight from Celie and her daughter Agnes. Soon my mother was squealing also. There were lots of hugs all around, and repeatedly I heard an ancient, thin voice crying, "My baby, my baby." Before I realized what was happening, I was out of the Buick myself and unexpectedly in the embrace of Aunt Celie. She was the oldest person I had ever touched. She squeezed me to her bony and wrinkled body. She was immaculately groomed, and she wore a starched white apron over her Sunday dress. Aunt Celie smelled of talcum powder, and her bare hands felt like fine leather gloves. Soon Agnes joined in the hugging, and the two of them alternated with choruses of "It's Joyce's boy! It's Baby's boy!" I felt absolutely overwhelmed. I also felt like a celebrity.

Soon we were inside the house. Other people, young and old, male and female, all African American, moved self-consciously in and out of the living room where we sat with Aunt Celie and Agnes. My impression was that all of these people were being headquartered in the kitchen and that each person was assigned his or her turn to come out and be introduced. There were lots of exclamations of "Growin' like a weed," "Hasn't changed a bit," and "Law me!" I was stunned by it all. Never before had I been so physically close to so many African American people. I had just been smothered with embraces from two black women out on the sidewalk, and now I was sitting in their home being introduced to what seemed like an army of other black people appearing from their kitchen.

As I remember it, Agnes had a deep, rich voice, and she was soon insisting that we must all have a little something to eat. Almost immediately, it seemed to me, the army of people, now all introduced, were streaming from the kitchen with coffee, cake, and lemonade. The cake was cut in thick slices. It was a marble cake, apparently a special treat prepared for my mother. It was served first to her, then to my father, uncle, and grandmother, then Agnes brought a piece of cake, a big piece, for me.

I sat silent, confused, and afraid with the cake, plate, napkin, and fork balanced on my lap. It seemed to me that everyone in the room was watching me and waiting for me to take a bite of the cake. I could not move. I felt frozen. I knew that I couldn't lift the cake to eat it, and I was frightened that if the plate started to slide off my lap, I wouldn't be able to move my hand to stop it. Take just a bite, try a little bit, taste Celie's cake, my mother and everyone else in the room seemed to be urging me, cajoling me. I couldn't eat the cake. The moment passed, the embarrassment waned, and the conversation moved on to other things. Later my mother quizzed me about the cake. I couldn't tell her why I wouldn't eat it—I honestly did not know myself. It took many years before I was able to reflect on my memory of that visit with Aunt Celie and decipher what it must have meant in my seven-year-old's grasp of people and relationships.

I did not eat the cake because it was made and served by "colored" people. I'm sure that is the correct word to use in describing my sense of the people who were trying so hard to be kind and hospitable to me. The people to whom I could not respond were colored. I'm certain that is the way I was thinking of Aunt Celie, Agnes, and the others that day. My parents did not use the term *colored* in the pejorative way that other, more hateful terms are used. While they were certainly products of the Southern culture of their own upbringing, they would not have used the other words with their children. They would not have been part of my vocabulary or of my way of thinking about people. No, I'm sure that *colored* would have been the word in my mind. I had not been taught to hate, but somehow I knew that there were cautions and limits necessary when dealing with colored people.

A song from the play *South Pacific* asserts that children must be carefully taught to hate and discriminate. I disagree. I think that prejudice is informally caught rather than formally taught. I think that by the time I was seven years old I had caught the belief from my social environment that black people were not to be touched or trusted. I think that I had already learned a sense of race and an ethic of racial separation. I cannot recall ever being taught them, but I know I had learned those lessons.

But what of my mother? Certainly she knew these things, but yet I had seen her allow herself to be embraced like a little girl by Aunt Celie and Agnes. Even more disturbing, she had returned their hugs with enthusiasm and obvious deep affection. She had not only eaten the marble cake, she had also tried to persuade me to do the same. It didn't make sense. I was soon relishing my other adventures in Montgomery, however, and remembering with pride how I sat behind the wheel of the hook and ladder truck at Uncle Ray's firehouse. The memories of the marble cake and Aunt Celie soon settled several layers below my consciousness.

In 1952, racial segregation in public schools was still the norm by law and/or practice in most parts of the United States. Racial separation in most areas of social life was an enforced standard. *Brown v. Board of Education*, in which the Supreme Court would rule that segregation in the public schools was unconstitutional, was still only being formulated in Topeka. Freedom rides and lunch counter protests were as yet undreamed expressions of the yearning for civil rights and personal dignity among America's black people. In Montgomery, where I rode the streets in my uncle's shiny black Buick, Rosa Parks was still sitting on the back seat of the bus or standing in its crowded aisle while seats at the front remained unfilled. The bus boycott that would occur there in a few years was as yet unthinkable. Martin Luther King, Jr., was an obscure young preacher.

Over the next twenty years and more, my memories of Aunt Celie were called up by events that stimulated once again what I experienced as a puzzling contradiction: Celie loved and was loved deeply by my mother, my mother respected and trusted Celie, yet I had learned that the right thing to do was to distance myself from people like Celie. How could it be that this woman evoked such behavior from my own mother? I recalled Aunt Celie throughout the events of the civil rights movement. I thought of her as I watched news reports of young black men and women being knocked to the ground with fire hoses and cursed by hate-filled white adults as they entered desegregated public schools. I saw her features in the faces of hundreds of elderly black people during my two years in the Peace Corps. Recognizing Aunt Celie's capacity for love and remembering my immature rejection of her have served as a challenge for growth and change throughout much of my life. I am deeply in her debt.

As I mentioned earlier, my mother told Carl and me stories of Aunt Celie before I met her in Montgomery. She also told the stories for years afterward. The stories were always the same. My grandmother ran a small neighborhood grocery store in Montgomery. She, my mother, and my uncles lived behind the store. The store had no name. It was nothing fancy. There was no electricity in the store and no indoor plumbing. They sold bologna, bread, crackers, beans, sugar, and other things that were considered staples at the time. Kerosene lamps were used for lighting, and clothes were washed in a tub with a scrub board. My mother washed clothes in the mornings before she went to school and pressed clothes using a charcoal-heated iron at night. She often talked of wearing clothes that other people had handed down to her. She explained that there was a woman her mama bought candy from for the store who had a girl a little older than she was, and that the woman would bring my mother her daughter's clothes.

Celie often went to their home behind the store. She brought a wooden box with her to sit on because she refused to sit on their furniture. My mother would sit on the floor; Celie sat on the box, brushed her hair, and told stories of her childhood in slavery. Aunt Celie and her mother were separated when she was very small. They were sold to different slaveholders. Her new mistress gave her a little perfume bottle to play with in an effort to comfort her. She stayed with this family as a slave until she was emancipated a few years later. She told my mother that her mistress was good to her. Aunt Celie treasured the perfume bottle for most of her life. She treasured it, but she treasured my mother more. She gave it to her baby as a gift of love.

I always assumed that Aunt Celie was hired by my grandmother to care for my mother. My grandmother raised four children without the help of a husband. I believed that Celie was probably paid to come in during times when my grandmother was most busy with the store. I must admit that there have been times when I have spoken reluctantly of Aunt Celie with other people because I thought her story would sound too much like a kindly black mammy tale about the woman who was hired to raise my mother, and what a loyal and loving servant she had been. A recent conversation with my mother, however, added a new dimension to my understanding of the relationship between her and Aunt Celie. Aunt Celie was not hired to care for my mother. She was instead a genuine friend and a kind neighbor who was in no sense employed to provide care. My grandmother's store was in a "colored" section of Montgomery. Most of her customers were black people. When my grandmother went into labor with my mother, she went to the back of the store to her bed. She sent one of my uncles for help. The local doctor could not be found, so she asked for Celie, whom by then she had known for some time. Celie came and, before Dr. Bickerstaff could be found, delivered my mother. For the rest of her life, she called my mother "my baby" or simply "Baby." It was a just claim. She literally brought my mother into the world.

Celie visited often with my mother in her home behind the store. My mother also visited Celie's home frequently. She remembers that Celie had a stereoscope, the antique forerunner of what some of us knew in childhood as a View-Master. She would sit for hours and look at cardboard pictures of dramatic scenes and faraway places. They talked, looked at the pictures through the stereoscope, and ate fresh figs from the tree in Aunt Celie's backyard. These were wonderful times for my mother, and she still becomes radiant when she describes them.

Prejudice is a form of mental illness—I'm convinced of it. Unfortunately, it is often a form of shared mania that results in causing great hurt to those who are the objects of its madness. Most people with other forms of mental illness are dangerous only to themselves. Prejudice is different. Its primary symptom is hatred of others, and those who are hated are at high risk for being hurt. Irrationally hating others because of their race, nationality, religion, gender, social class, or any other characteristic can become all-consuming. Such irrationality has repeatedly proven itself to be resistant to all reason and to all evidence contrary to its poisoned convictions.

Prejudice, however, has often been elevated and dignified by powerful and influential people who have supported it in the name of reason and have advanced it in the name of science. There have been scientific assaults on people because of their social class or racial identity. Laws and practices have been aimed at controlling the lives of people deemed inferior because of race or class. Claims have been made for a scientific basis for those laws and practices. The illness of prejudicial thought can infect the intellect at what we consider its highest levels and in what we think of as its purest forms. Many people in law, medicine, science, and human services have been convinced that they have the right and responsibility to intervene in powerful and intimate ways in the lives of other people for their own good and for the protection of society. People have been hurt by what was done to them in the name of scientific, medical, or political necessity.

Our culture is even more socially complex and confusing today than it was in our past. Confusion and complexity, however, should not seduce us into engaging in simple and expedient actions that rob others of their liberty and dignity. Prejudice must be struggled against continually. I don't think that you can simply overcome a bad case of it or that you can inoculate a child for life against ever catching it. It is all around us, and I believe that the challenge is to examine each day the assumptions that we make about other people and the fear of people we harbor because of the way they look, speak, worship, or otherwise live their lives. Just when you think you have overcome a prejudicial view, you find yourself on one of those dark, lonely streets of life and the complexion of the stranger coming toward you makes a difference in the degree of your discomfort.

In a world filled with negative, and all too often evil, abstractions about people who are different from oneself, I have found comfort and reassurance in concrete human interactions. My relationships with people from diverse cultural and ethnic backgrounds have taught me much about dignity in human life. Some of my most profound lessons about freedom have come from knowing people who have been oppressed because they came from a particular minority group. When I am tempted to allow race to become something negative in my thinking, I remember Aunt Celie. I recall her embracing my mother on the sidewalk as I watched in Montgomery that afternoon in 1952, and I imagine the day years before when she gently bathed a newborn with love.

Several times during the last few years, I have asked my mother about the perfume bottle. I remember seeing it as a child, and the image I have is of a small glass vial with a metal filigree covering. Each time I have asked about it, she has replied evasively that it is put away somewhere and that she will try to find it sometime before my next visit. Somehow, the next time I ask it has slipped her mind, and it is just too late or she is too busy to look for it just then. I suspect that the bottle is wrapped carefully in flannel cloth scraps in a box that once held Christmas cards. I imagine that it has been placed safely under rarely used things in a dresser drawer. I also suspect that it has become too precious to share when the house is filled with activity and grandchildren. I understand. And I have memories. That is all that matters.

5

Lessons in Patois

Learning to Be a Jamaican

The inauguration of President John F. Kennedy, and his inspiring speeches and his youthful leadership, are memories that have been vivid in my mind since I was an adolescent. Although some of the dreams of social reform of those years have clearly failed us, and some of the hopes of that time have become tarnished, I still cherish the energy and optimism that Kennedy brought to our country. Although the influence that some of the people and events of those years have had on my personal and professional life has ebbed and waned, one of the ideals of those days, service to others, became central to my identity.

In a sense, my adult awareness of the relationship among politics, leadership, and social issues began with the Kennedy presidency, but it all seemed threatened by his sudden and meaningless assassination. Watching the casket-bearing caisson, the lone prancing horse, little John John's salute, and the procession of mourners in the streets brought to my mind questions of whether, indeed, the dreams would die with the dreamer. The dreams were crystallized anew, however, with the campaign of the president's brother Robert. Listening to Bobby Kennedy's speeches of commitment and resolve convinced me that the dreams could be kept alive.

The year after Bobby's murder and the assassination of Martin Luther King, my wife Joyce and I decided to be part of the dream that remained alive. We joined the Peace Corps. This had been a goal for both of us that began in high school when we listened to John Kennedy's description of a "moral equivalent of war." We continued to want to be part of that effort, and after we finished college and married, we submitted our Peace Corps applications with visions of being called to serve in Africa or South America.

When the call came, however, it was to an unexpected part of the world. We were invited to enter Peace Corps training for two years of service in Jamaica. All that I knew of Jamaica when the invitation came was rum, the limbo, and, vaguely, a new kind of music called reggae. My stereotypic images of the country were simply those of a would-be Caribbean tourist. Soon, however, I learned of a Jamaica that most people, even those who have visited its tourist beaches, have not heard of or seen.

The Jamaica I discovered as I read the Peace Corps literature was a third world nation struggling to feed, clothe, house, and educate its people. It was a nation of people with a sense of cultural pride but little else. Economically, it was one of the poorest nations in the Western Hemisphere. It was a country striving to define itself out of the vestiges of slavery and colonialism.

Joyce and I joined the Peace Corps in June, 1969. It was an exciting experience for us as we left everything we were accustomed to and flew to California for our initial orientation and training. We were soon caught up in the energy of becoming part of a group of about a hundred people who, for varied reasons, shared our dream of the Peace Corps. We were a diverse group. Most of us were young, but there were several people in their forties and fifties. There were even a few retirees. There seemed to be only two common denominators in our group. First, we all seemed to have a sense of the hope of somehow making a "difference." But there was something else—we also seemed to have a sense of adventure that blended well with that idealism. As we came to know each other, that blend became even more apparent. We were not self-sacrificing martyrs. We were concerned people, but we were also individuals who enjoyed new experiences, new people, and new ideas. When I looked back later on those people who did not make it through the training, and some of those who did not complete the entire two years, I found that in a number of cases part of the blend was missing. The idealism and commitment to service was there, but the sense of adventure that helps sustain a person through such commitments was missing. I think that the same blend required for the Peace Corps may be needed for teaching. Teaching requires a belief in and commitment to ideals. Teachers, however, must be sustained in their work by their enjoyment of adventure and risk-taking. It takes both idealism and adventurousness for a career as daring and demanding as that of an educator.

Each day of training brought new insights and adventures to us. One morning we were taken to the Mexican border at Tijuana, given a map of places to find and a dollar, and told to be back at the border by 7:00 that evening. Another time, we were placed in an urban ghetto for several weeks so that we would have the experience of being in the minority in an unwelcoming environment. We were scolded by Black Panther intellectuals who questioned our motivations as "do-gooders." They challenged us to stay at home and do something about the racism in our own neighborhoods and the poverty in our own country. We were examined and tested in detail for psychological and medical problems that might interfere with being able to serve in a positive role for two years in a country so different from our own. We were immunized against various diseases, even for some diseases that had never been detected in the hemisphere let alone in Jamaica. We were exposed to new diets, a new history, and a new way of thinking about our own competencies. We were also cautioned not to expect to accomplish major transformations. "Small gains" seemed to be the prevailing message from those who did their best to prepare us for our lives as volunteers.

Just as Joyce and I were gaining confidence in our abilities to complete the training and serve successfully as volunteers, we were thrown an unexpected curve. A decision was made that I should go to Jamaica early and that she would follow with most of the other volunteers in three weeks. My assignment was to be working with teachers on better understanding child development and teaching children with special needs. It was decided that I would benefit most from the remaining weeks of training by being in Jamaica and learning about the schools, families, and culture of the community where I would be living. Joyce would be working with preschool teachers. She was to remain in California, in an excellent training program for those going into preschool education in developing countries. She would join me when she and the other volunteers had completed that training. We were disappointed, but we understood the reason for the separation. I left one evening with a few other volunteers who were also being sent to Jamaica early, and we arrived in Kingston the following evening. It was the day of the first moon landing. I listened to the words of Neil Armstrong as I sat on the veranda of the home of a Jamaican Ministry of Education official. She explained to me that many of the "country folks" in Jamaica did not believe that Americans were really landing on the moon. The night before she had heard a fisherman say that Americans couldn't be landing on the moon because the moon was in Jamaica that evening, "Look 'bov your head mon. It right there. You see any Americans?"

The next morning I was on my way to meet lots of "country folks." I was taken to the village where Joyce and I would live for the next two years. I was excited, and a little intimidated, when I was dropped off at the home of a teacher who had agreed to give me room and board until I could find a place for us to live. I was immediately made to feel a part of the family, however, and was instructed on how to eat ackee and saltfish, curried goat, and boiled green bananas. I was also given a lesson in the proper way to drink white rum (straight, chased with water).

After breakfast on my first morning in the village, I walked around my new neighborhood. People were friendly. I am certain that most of them

Connection

thought that I was a tourist who had strayed from the usual tourist haunts. Eventually, I reached the market at the center of town. People were gathered around the edges of a large open area selling fish, vegetables, fruits, and an assortment of clothing and household items. I enjoyed looking at the items that people had spread on the ground in front of them. I was mistaken for a tourist several times and offered special deals on trinkets. I finally gave in to one very persistent woman who said that I needed a hat to "put shade 'pon you." Actually, I liked the straw hat a lot. It was the kind of hat I had seen a number of Jamaican men wearing, and I thought it gave me a distinctly nontourist look. I soon learned, however, that it was not convincing.

After putting on my new hat, I started walking across the open area of the market square. As I walked, I heard a strong clear voice calling out, "Why are you here? This is not your place; this is not your place. Why are you here?" I saw immediately that it was the voice of a man with a long beard and dreadlocks. He was a Rastafarian of about fifty. He carried a long staff, and he had a cloth bag slung over one shoulder. Again he called out, "This is not your place" and this time it was obvious that he was yelling to me. I continued to walk across the square and tried to ignore his calls. I noticed, however, that activity had stopped in the market and people were watching me. I wanted to disappear. I decided, however, that since this was my first day in the place that would be my home for two years, I had better respond to the man. I thought I should try to understand what he was saying to me. I walked over to him, attempting to hide my fear, and asked him if he was talking to me.

The man's eyes were clear and piercing. He seemed to look straight through me and then explained, "This is not your place, this is not a place for tourists. You belong somewhere else. This is a market for Jamaican people."

Rastafarians are keenly aware of the psychology and sociology of slavery and colonialism that continues to keep people in bondage even after they have been politically emancipated. They were among the earliest of the people who promoted black pride and a sense of connectedness to their African cultural and religious roots. They have found dignity in separating themselves from what they think has tainted the lives of people of African descent. At that moment I did not fully understand this. That was why, however, this man was telling me that he thought I didn't belong in his village, that it was not good for me to be there.

I paused for a moment and then responded to him that I was not a tourist. "I have come here to live for a while," I said. "I am a Peace Corps Volunteer." The man seemed to ponder my comment for a few moments. He also seemed to be studying my face again with his piercing eyes. I would later learn that he understood very well the mission of the Peace Corps. I would learn, in fact, that his understanding of the government, history, and politics of the United States was quite astute. But after a few more moments he asked quite simply, "What is your mission here with the Peace Corps?"

During our training we examined this question repeatedly, asking ourselves: What am I trying to do? For Jamaicans? For myself? For my own country? Why am I doing this? Ideals? Adventure? Escape? Some of these questions raced through my mind as I formulated my response to his question, but none of them seemed to matter at the moment. I replied, "I have come here to be a teacher." Immediately he asked, "Who will you teach, Teacher?" I explained that I would be working with Jamaican teachers and that I would also be teaching Jamaican children.

The questions that came next from the man in dreadlocks have remained fixed in my memory for over thirty years. He again looked me directly in the eyes and asked, "What will you teach them, Teacher, how to be Americans? We need our children to be strong Jamaicans. Can you teach them that?"

I was stunned by his questions, and I had no answers to them. I muttered something about teaching reading and writing, and other skills, but my response was not satisfying even to me. We talked a little longer, the circle of people around us who had been listening to our conversation dispersed, and we parted ways for the day. For weeks, however, I was haunted by his questions and sought for myself the answers to them. What would I teach the children other than reading and writing? What did I know that I could teach them that would help them be strong Jamaicans?

During my years in Jamaica I revisited those questions many times and found many different answers to them. During that time I also found a friend in the Rastafarian who had called to me with questions about why I was in his village. He was known by everyone in the village as Tennie. He was also known to many as a wild man who could spend the better part of any day lecturing loudly to the people in the market about his most recent political, religious, or economic concern. I came to understand that he enjoyed debating issues with anyone who took him seriously and that he was actually very open to the ideas of others. He was, in fact, one of the most intellectually active and insightful people that I have ever met. He was also passionately concerned about his country.

As I became more acclimated to the culture and language of Jamaica, I found that I could more easily follow conversations in the market, and along the roads, that were incomprehensible to me when I first arrived. The official language of Jamaica is English. It is the official language of instruction in the schools, and all government and business is conducted in English. The language spoken as the most common social and personal means of expression, however, is Patois (pronounced PAT-wah). Patois is a blend of English, a number of African dialects, and many words and expressions of uniquely Jamaican origin. There is no written form of Patois, so the only way to learn it is to be immersed in it.

Even though my work with teachers and children was in English, I heard them speaking Patois on the playground and at other informal moments. I heard Patois as I traveled the roads between schools, and I heard it in the market. I also heard Patois at the little store (a "shop" to Jamaicans) where I sometimes stopped for hard bread and cheese and something cold to drink on my way home at the end of the day. It was in that little shop that I decided to make my first public try at speaking Patois.

One afternoon as I was sitting in the shop eating my bread and cheese and sipping my ginger beer, a child I had worked with that day in her school entered with her mother. She did not see me at first, but when she did, I greeted her with "Whapon" and a few other words in Patois. Immediately, her mother took her by the hand and fled from the shop. The owner, Mr. Peachel, looked at me in disbelief and said, "Forgive me, Teacher, but I must tell you that you insulted that mother and her child." I asked if I had said something the wrong way, with the wrong inflection perhaps, that had made my Patois expression of greeting come out insulting. "No, Teacher, they understood you. But you must not speak Patois to the children. You are a teacher, and you are an American. The mother thought you were speaking down to her child as if she couldn't understand English." I understood then that my use of Patois with the child was as unnatural as if I had attempted to use an African American dialect to a child and mother in United States.

I eventually came to use Patois in my personal relationships. As I came to know fishermen who beached their boats and mended their nets near our home, Patois became a natural part of our conversations. Late night conversations with my Jamaican education friends were often facilitated by good Jamaican rum and filled with Patois expressions. In fact, those friends delighted in my use of these expressions and my increasing under-standing of the Jamaican "inside jokes" that came to me with time. They would sometimes remark that I was "becoming a Jamaican."

I believe that in some ways I did become a Jamaican and still am. The drawing that hangs on my office wall of a Jamaican woman and her infant (a Jamaican Madonna) is one of my most treasured objects. Tennie also thought I had become a Jamaican, and we both knew that we had become friends. I have a large photograph of him that he reluctantly consented to when a Jamaican friend of ours asked to take his picture. I treasure it also.

During the time we were in the Peace Corps, Joyce and I missed the spectacle of Woodstock and the tragedy of Kent State. We returned to the United States in 1971 to a country that had changed dramatically. We had also undergone a transformation.

In addition to becoming a little bit of a Jamaican during those years, I think I also learned a great deal about teaching that has been central to my life as an educator. I learned that I wasn't there to teach the children to become Americans. I learned that I was there to teach them what I could that would enable them to have choices in their lives. I was there to teach them to understand as much as possible about their history and circum-stances so that they could make their own decisions about where they wanted to go and what they wanted to become. I was there to help teach them the joy and excitement of learning. In answer to Tennie's question, I hope that in this sense I helped a few of them become stronger Jamaicans.

These insights have also guided my work with people with disabilities. They have helped me understand that my roles as teacher and counselor are not intended to make children and adults with special needs "into" something else. My efforts with them are not focused on achieving a goal of "normality." Our mission together, on the contrary, is to help them to achieve greater strength and to increase their options while honoring their unique and individual values. Thanks for the help, Tennie.

6

A Father's Proud Moment

The Day My Daughter
Became a Gifted Samaritan

"Daddy, what are you going to do about it?" my daughter Allison asked me, referring to the problem of homelessness. It was 1987 and we were on vacation in New York City. My wife, Joyce, and I had looked forward for a long time to introducing our three children to the city. We had lived there while studying and working at Columbia University, and we had many treasured memories that we wanted to revisit and share with our children, Link, Allison, and Sallie.

In the decade since we had lived in the city, however, New York had been faced with greater challenges than ever before. Changes in federal policies and programs had manifested themselves most visibly among the urban poor. There were many more homeless, confused, and disenfranchised people on the streets of New York than we had ever seen before. My children had learned the term *street people* as an abstraction. Now, as we walked the streets of the city, they connected that term with the real people they saw sleeping on the pavement, rummaging through garbage, or walking about disoriented and clearly impoverished.

Allison, who was seven, was particularly moved by what she saw, and asked if I thought that one man, who looked alarmingly dirty, ill, and exhausted, would die. I answered that unless something happened, unless he got help soon, he probably would. That was when she asked what I have come to call "Allison's question": "Daddy, what are you going to do about it?"

Joyce and I, like most parents, have tried to teach our children to do the "right thing" in relation to other people. Again, like most other parents, we try to teach our children by example, modeling that other people must be treated with care and respect. At least we hope that we have provided this example. Therefore, I took Allison's question as a positive sign: She had come to expect her parents to try to help people who need it. At seven, however, she also believed that her mother and I had the ability to do whatever needed to be done to help others. She believed we could always "make things better."

On that street in New York, however, I was inarticulate in answering Allison's question. As I stumbled and stammered my way around her concern, the best I could do was to tell her that it's not possible for us to directly help everyone in need. I talked about how our contributions to our church and to charities help people like the man she was so concerned about. Allison was not satisfied with this answer. I was also immediately embarrassed to have offered it to my child. The moment passed, but my discomfort did not.

In the story of the Good Samaritan, the two men who passed by the sufferer without helping him crossed to the other side of the road when they saw him. Not only would they not help, they also avoided being near the suffering man. These men were probably not unfeeling and inhumane. They simply did not want to risk becoming involved. Perhaps they were family men with responsibilities to others that they felt took precedence. Maybe they were afraid of being tricked and finding themselves victims of attack and robbery. They may have been wary of becoming involved with someone who would require more and more of them. And so, they walked to the other side of the road to avoid even seeing the hurting man whom they felt they could not help.

Months passed before I spoke with Allison again about her question. Finally, I was able to talk with her about the limits to what one person can do in helping others. In addition, recalling the parable of the Good Samaritan, I explained to Allison that, although her mother and I could not help everyone who needed help, we did care. I promised her that, even though seeing a need one cannot meet is painful, we will always see others and their needs and care about them. I explained that what is most important is that we not walk to the other side of the road, that we not avoid seeing the needs of others even when we can't meet them immediately. We talked, and I believe she understood what I was trying to say.

The philosopher Judith Jarvis Thomson, in discussing the murder of Kitty Genovese decades ago in New York City, revisited the story of the Good Samaritan. Kitty Genovese was repeatedly and brutally attacked, and finally murdered, while thirty-eight people watched from their apartments and did nothing to help her. Thomson said that a Good Samaritan would have rushed out, risking death in an attempt to help. Such a person, she said, would be not just *good* but a *Splendid Samaritan!* In fact, however, not one of the thirty-eight witnesses even picked up a telephone to call the police, an action that would have caused them no danger. Calling the police, Thomson said, would have been the act of a *Minimally Decent Samaritan.* Thomson's observation has made an important impact on my view of many of our contemporary social problems. What we need to make a decent society is not a few Splendid Samaritans but millions of Minimally Decent Samaritans. We all need to strive for greater decency in the ways that we treat each other.

Two years after our New York trip, while visiting Allison's elementary school, I was again confronted with her question and, this time, with her insights on that question. She was nearing the end of the third grade, and I was on a routine mission: I was bringing a forgotten lunch bag to school.

As I entered the hallway, her teacher, Ms. Vaughan, was closing her classroom door behind her. She seemed a little more surprised to see me than usual, and she hesitated for a moment as she took the lunch bag. She explained that she had something important to tell me.

The afternoon before had apparently been very traumatic for some of the children in Allison's class. The announcement of the selection of children for the gifted program had been made. Only one child from her class made the list. The elementary gifted program in this system included a pull-out program for the fourth grade. Students selected for the program spent these years at the "GO" Center. They rejoined their peers at middle school two years later. Ms. Vaughan explained, as she took the brown bag from me, that Allison had been her clear choice for the GO program. A boy in the class, however, had higher test scores and, on that basis, had been picked by the selection committee. She was very apologetic and uneasy until I explained that it was not a big deal for us. In fact, had Allison been selected I was doubtful that we would have wanted her to leave her peers and the school she loved so much—even for two years of accelerated and enriched programming. We were pleased with the education Allison was receiving, and I didn't think we would have traded it for something so different.

Ms. Vaughan smiled and said she had something special to share with me. That morning two girls in the class had been quite upset. One felt that her parents were terribly disappointed that she was not selected for the gifted program. Both the mother and the father were highly competitive and high-achieving people. Their daughter felt she had let them down by not being "number one." The other girl was also afraid that she had disappointed her parents. She had an older brother who had been selected for the program several years earlier.

Ms. Vaughan had found both girls being comforted by Allison. Allison was assuring them that not being selected for the program was no disaster. She had also consoled them by saying, "It is more important that we will all be together next year. I would rather be a Samaritan than be in the GO program. Good Samaritans stick together and help each other. We are really Good Samaritans. My Dad says it is better to be a Good Samaritan than to be rich or famous."

Ms. Vaughan explained to me that the comforting that Allison had offered the other girls had worked. They both seemed to be feeling better. I explained to the teacher that I couldn't be prouder of my daughter. Allison had shared a rare and precious gift.

I read an excellent book not long ago by William F. May called *The Patient's Ordeal*. In his introduction to the book, May describes an exchange that T.S. Eliot had with a college student. Eliot had given a lecture on some serious problem in American life. During the question-and-answer period following the lecture, the student asked urgently, "Mr. Eliot, what are we going to do about the problem you have discussed?" Eliot replied to the student, "You have asked the wrong question. You must understand that we face two types of problems in life. One kind of problem provokes the question, 'What are we going to do about it?' The other kind poses the subtler question, 'How do we behave toward it?'"

It seems clear to me that the first kind of problem can be solved with direct, sometimes simple, and immediate action. The immediate relief that a doctor or dentist can give a patient is an example of this kind of problem resolution. The second kind of problem is a greater challenge. This is a problem that has no direct, simple, or immediate solution. What do you do for a dying friend or family member? Do you avoid the person because you cannot cure his or her suffering or prevent the inevitable? A loving response to your friend or relative in such a situation requires a different approach to the problem: You must see it as another opportunity to show caring in an enduring relationship.

When I initially tried to respond to Allison's question—"What are you going to do about it?"—I sought a fast and clean solution to the problem of protecting and seeking the well-being of another human being. I understand now that he needed more than a "quick fix" to his problems: He needed a sense of connectedness to his culture that would endure. I suspect that this is the greatest need of many of our fellow human beings. The simple problems that can be fixed quickly are not the ones that drain us. Having people who will endure with us is one of the greatest of our human needs. It is a gift of great value. Schools that promote this kind of caring are helping to educate truly gifted students.

7

Recapturing the Spirit of Caring

Uncle, Brownie, and Sausage Biscuits

An uncle can be a very special person to a child. At times he may be nurturing and protective in a way that supplements or, in some cases, substitutes for the love of a father. He may also be a close friend or big brother to a boy or girl who needs one. An uncle might also be a man who allows a child to see the world through the eyes of another male, someone beside the father; he may broaden the vision of life's possibilities that a good father has already provided.

My Uncle Ganiel was the kind of man who made the world more interesting and exciting for me as a boy growing up in Virginia in the 1950s. He was a big man with a bold voice. He walked and talked with bravado, and he made me laugh. He kidded me in a way that I always knew expressed affection. Over the years, he joked with me about girls, about remembering me as a toddler who used to have accidents in his pants, and about being too tall and skinny as an adolescent. He had rusty hair and freckles on his arms. He appeared to be strong against the world's stings, but I often saw his eyes puddle with tears when he spoke of children in need. More than once I was aware that he bought groceries for a family in trouble. He had them delivered anonymously.

From the time of my earliest recollections, I called him Uncle, just Uncle. I continued to call him Uncle until he died. I think he enjoyed being called by that name. Maybe it reminded him of the earlier days of our relationship, when I was a child and he was a young man. I miss Uncle greatly. It is hard to accept death when it comes to one so full of life.

Uncle liked to hunt. One of my early memories is of a deer's head mounted on the wall of Uncle's living room. The antlers were shiny with shellac and the fur was stiff. But it was the brown glass eyes that were a source of amazement and intimidation to a four-year-old. They seemed to follow me wherever I walked in the room. I remember being afraid of staying alone in the room with the head. If Uncle was in the room, however, I felt safe.

Uncle owned a small hunting cabin. It was actually a house trailer that he had covered with a zinc roof and to which he had added a porch. It was located on a few acres of land in a very secluded forest area. A beautiful mountain creek ran by it. Every fall Uncle went to his cabin during deer season for a few days. He would meet there with some of his friends and sometimes with his son, my cousin Orbie. One of his best friends had a cabin on an adjoining lot. It was a time for renewing and strengthening friendships, but I am not sure how much hunting was actually done. In fact I am not sure how many deer Uncle ever killed or wanted to kill. The only one I saw evidence of was the trophy with glass eyes in his living room.

In addition to being with his friends, hunting was important to Uncle for another reason. It was a good excuse for having a dog. Over the years, Uncle had a series of dogs that started out as working animals or strays and ended up as beloved friends to him. Each seemed to come to him by appearing out of a storm or after having been abandoned along an isolated road. In every case, however, Uncle found a special feature of the dog that was worthy of repeated praise. His dog was always the smartest dog he had ever known, or the fastest dog he had ever seen, or the sweetest animal that he had ever seen around children. The first of Uncle's dogs that I remember was Brownie. I have a vivid image of Brownie lying on the wide wooden porch that wrapped around the house that Uncle shared with my Aunt Catherine, Orbie, and my younger cousin, Lisa. Brownie seemed to always be there sleeping in the sun while, as Uncle assured me, he was also doing his work of protecting the house. Actually, I don't think I ever heard Brownie bark at anyone or anything. Uncle once explained that Brownie was getting old and had already done his share of the world's work. He had been, according to Uncle, the best hunting dog he had ever seen. I'm not sure if that was true, but I always believed that Brownie had been the dog that flushed the deer on Uncle's wall out of the woods. I'm inclined to believe today that it was the only deer that either of them ever needed. I think of the deer on the wall as a symbol of the bond between Uncle and Brownie that was complete in itself, no further evidence of their shared hunting adventures was required.

I have wonderful memories of visits to Uncle's house as a child and teenager. Aunt Catherine always went out of her way to make me feel at home, Lisa was full of fun, and Orbie was inevitably involved in a project that fascinated me. He is a few years older, and he taught me much about history, art, and philosophy through the model ships and planes that he constructed, the music he listened to, and the books that he talked about. At meals, Uncle consistently told me that I didn't eat "enough to keep a bird alive," but he also let me know that I didn't have to eat anything that I didn't want to eat. Uncle himself had interesting dietary preferences. I don't remember a single time that pinto beans were not served at lunch and dinner by Aunt Catherine. She once told me that Uncle had asked for pintos on their wedding day, and that since that first day of her married life she had always kept a pot of beans on the stove. She explained that he had grown up in a large family where pintos were the staple that enabled the family to be fed adequately day in and day out. Aunt Catherine also usually had mashed potatoes on the table at every noon and evening meal. Fresh cornbread or slices of "whitebread" were common, and during the summer, sliced tomatoes and green beans rounded out the meals that I now think of with great pleasure.

I do not remember ever seeing Uncle eat meat at lunch or dinner. Aunt Catherine explained to me that this was because meat had been so expensive and scarce in Uncle's family while he was growing up in rural poverty. Indeed, I remember when Uncle came to our house one afternoon to pick up Aunt Catherine. She had been visiting with us for the morning. He had not had anything to eat since breakfast, yet he declined my mother's offers of leftover fried chicken or anything else in our kitchen he might want. He made his own inventory of the contents of the refrigerator. He then proceeded to fix a sandwich of cold mashed potatoes on the heal slices from a loaf of bread. The experience of watching Uncle eating a cold mashed potato sandwich made quite an impression on me!

Uncle was not a vegetarian. The first time I remember seeing Uncle eat meat, however, was on an early morning ride I took with him. It was in the pickup truck that he used in his work for a hardware company. The night before, he, Aunt Catherine, Orbie, Lisa, and I had squeezed into the truck cab for a ride to buy ice cream cones. In the process of getting in and trying to get settled, however, I left my hand in the hinge as the door was slammed shut. The pain was awful. I cried and felt panic. Immediately, my fingernails turned purple. Soon we were back in the house. Aunt Catherine carefully soaked and bandaged my fingers. Uncle paced and cussed at fate, at the truck, and perhaps even at himself. I knew, however, it was not directed at me.

The next morning Uncle offered to give me another ride in his truck. I don't remember where Aunt Catherine, Orbie, and Lisa were, but I do remember that Uncle and I took Brownie and went for a ride. By this time, Brownie was both blind and arthritic. Uncle had to help him into the truck.

Soon Brownie was curled up on the floorboard. As we drove through the quiet streets of Roanoke, Virginia, Uncle asked me if my fingers still hurt. He told me to be sure to keep soaking them regularly until the swelling, which was now very obvious, went down.

Uncle pulled the pickup into the parking lot of a diner that was a local legend. It was one of those places that during the fifties and sixties sold hamburgers that were about the size of half dollars. They were sold for about fifteen cents each. For fifty cents you could buy four. In the mornings the same deal was offered for "sausageburgers" of the same size. Uncle parked the truck, went into the diner, and soon returned with a bag. He insisted that I have two of the sandwiches. He had only one. The fourth sausage sandwich was served to Brownie on the floor of the truck's cab. Although it took Brownie a moment to catch on, he really appreciated that burger once he recognized the bun and meat for what it was. Almost apologizing for giving the sandwich to a dog, Uncle told me that he thought it was important to remember that "an old dog like Brownie deserves to have a friend."

Uncle and Aunt Catherine lived modestly. They were not people who wasted things or indulged themselves, let alone a pet. Uncle wanted me to know that the sausageburger for Brownie was special. Brownie finished the sausage but left some of the bread. Uncle drove us back to the house in silence. I will always remember that brief ride. By taking me on this special trip, he had shown me in a simple way that he cared about me, and he had allowed me to see him caring about Brownie. I also gained some other new insights into the beauty and depth of his character.

Uncle's last dog was named Benji. The two of them rode everywhere together in Uncle's car and were pretty much inseparable friends in most other respects. Among their rituals was an early morning ride and visit to the drive-thru at a local fast food franchise. The days of the old diner and sausageburgers had, of course, given way to sausage biscuits at Hardee's. Because of his health problems, he could no longer eat sausage or the rich biscuits that the patties were served on. His trip to the drive-thru was just for Benji. Apparently, the workers at the Hardee's window looked forward each morning to seeing the dog sitting up with what they thought looked like a grin on his face in anticipation of his breakfast.

I once asked Uncle about Benji and his breakfast trips. He told me that it meant more to him to see his dog enjoying those sausage biscuits than if he were still able to eat them himself. He said that it was the same kind of feeling that he got when he saw something good happening for one of his grandchildren—it felt better than if it were happening for him. He said that "after a certain point in life you have had enough of almost everything for yourself, and then the best times for you are when you see children and young people made happy by the little things you can do for them. And it's the same with Benji and his biscuits too." He added, "Of course there has never been another dog quite like Benji."

I was a pallbearer at Uncle's funeral. I left for the funeral early and stopped for coffee at the Hardee's where Uncle and Benji had made their morning visits. I sat and thought of the years I had known Uncle and the good things that he had done for me. He had made me feel important by giving his attention to me, even through his joking and kidding. He had taught me some important lessons about life by letting me see some of the sensitive and tender parts of his character. I knew that he was always glad to see me. I miss him, but he lives on in my heart through my many warm memories of him. I'm glad and proud that he was my Uncle.

Eminent developmental psychologist Erik Erikson described four overarching tasks of adult life. He felt that for an adult to have lived out his or her best potentials and possibilities, it is necessary that the life span of that person include: the development of an independent sense of identity, the achievement of the capacity to be truly intimate and committed in relationships, and the ability to be wise and insightful about the temporary nature of one's own life and the achievement of peace concerning death. A fourth task of life that he considered critical to adult development is the capacity for what he called *generativity.* He used the term in part to describe parents' nurturing of a new generation, through which they discover new ways of caring for others. Through the experience of nurturing children, we may gain a new sense of the joy of giving and the meaningfulness of making sacrifices for others. Erikson felt, however, that we become generative not only with our own children but in the many ways that as adults we may care for extended families, neighbors, communities, churches or temples, and even other people's children.

My memories of Uncle serve as an example for me of what it means to be generative. His model of finding simple joy in the nurturance of others, even greater joy than in finding rewards for himself, is encouraging to me. I believe that this is the essence of being "grown up." Maturity means being more engaged in the growth and benefit of others who need your help than you are involved in activities for your own personal gain. Erikson, in fact, described the opposite of generativity as self-absorption or stagnation. He felt that the adult who is unable to become generative becomes so self-focused that he or she is incapable of the joy of maturity. This is a person who spends time and energy in a continuing attempt to seek gratification for self and to ease the pain of a lonely existence through self-absorption.

Uncle's happiness in seeing the joy of others has also caused me to reflect upon our society as a whole. I have come to believe that we as a nation must recapture a sense of the generativity that characterized our ideals in the past. We as a nation must "grow up" enough again to look outward for the gratification of helping others to learn, to be healthier, to be more secure, to have better living conditions. The most fortunate among us have sought wealth, power, independence, and pleasure for ourselves and have found it. It is incumbent upon us now, if we are to be a truly generative nation, that we face the poverty, homelessness, discouragement, and hopelessness in those all around us and find true gratification in helping others, those with disabilities and those with other special needs, to find nourishment, shelter, opportunities for growth, and belief in themselves. It is critical to our health as a culture that we become a more caring and inclusive community.

Part I
Questions to Ponder

1. What memories from your own childhood do you have that have most influenced your adult perceptions of people with disabilities?

2. Do you believe that adult vocational choices are often influenced by particular childhood and adolescent experiences or events? Can you think of examples of this from your own life or from the lives of relatives or friends?

3. Do you think that certain experiences bring about sudden and dramatic changes in our attitudes and actions toward other people? Or, do you think that we are molded by the gradual accumulation of experiences? Both?

4. Is there a Mike, Nan, or Tiny in your life? Can you tell the story of that relationship and its effect on you?

5. Did an adult like Uncle, Aunt Celie, or Tennie help you gain a new perspective on human differences and need? Can you tell the story of your experience with that person?

Part II

Disability, Science, and Pseudoscience

Burton Blatt once wrote concerning the importance of stories, "Every story can enhance a life or destroy it. Every story can lift us or depress us. Stories sustain if not make a person's world. And thus, the storyteller holds a certain power and responsibility" (Blatt, 1987, p. 141).

This is certainly true in very important ways with regard to stories of disability. Heroic stories like that of Helen Keller and Annie Sullivan have encouraged parents and professionals who care deeply about children and adults with disabilities. Often, however, the nature and intent of disability stories have been negative.

The stories of eugenics and feeblemindness examined in this part of *In Search of Better Angels*, for example, questioned the need for and efficacy of providing education and social services for people identified as mentally retarded. In particular, the story of Carrie Buck became central to arguments for the necessity for institutionalizing and sterilizing thousands of people labeled with the term.

In the autumn of 1927, Charles Lindbergh was completing a hero's tour of the United States in celebration of his transatlantic flight. On October 19, he landed at Logan Field in Baltimore. During a ticker tape parade through the city, office workers craned their necks from windows to see the "Lone Eagle," America's hero of the day. The crowds were so thick that police had difficulty keeping the streets open for the motorcade.

On the same day in Lynchburg, Virginia, another historic event was taking place. For this one there would be no parade, no ticker tape, and no hero. At the State Colony for Epileptics and Feebleminded, a young woman named Carrie Buck was being sexually sterilized. Without her comprehending what was being done to her, and without her consent, her capacity to have children was taken away.

The operation was performed in the name of eugenics and with the sanction of the U.S. Supreme Court. It was done with the claim that Carrie Buck was "mentally defective." Over time this claim was proven wrong, and it became evident that Carrie had been selected to test the constitutionality of Virginia's sterilization law because she was powerless. Fifty years later when reporters asked Carrie Buck how she had felt, she replied, "They just told me I had to have an operation, that was all" (Smith & Nelson, 1989, p. xviii).

The eugenic stories presented here portray abuses of power in the name of science and social necessity. They are also intended to convey the need for caution, clarity, and care in the ways we portray and treat people who appear to us to be different in some significant way from ourselves.

REFERENCES AND FURTHER READINGS

Blatt, B. (1987). *The conquest of mental retardation.* Austin, TX: Pro-Ed.
Smith, J. D., & Nelson, K. (1989). *The sterilization of Carrie Buck.* Far Hills, NJ: New Horizon Press.

8

Eugenics,
Old and New

Mensa and the Human Genome Project

THE TRAGEDY OF
INVOLUNTARY STERILIZATION

In 1927, a young woman named Carrie Buck was sterilized. She was the first person under a Virginia law to be subjected to surgery that had been declared constitutional by the U.S. Supreme Court. It allowed the sterilization of men and women judged to be psychologically or socially incompetent. Carrie Buck had been committed to an institution and diagnosed as "feeble-minded." The commitment followed the birth of her illegitimate child.

Although Carrie Buck was not the first person to be involuntarily sterilized, she was the first to have the surgery performed with the legitimizing power of a Supreme Court decision. After her operation, thousands of other people were sterilized under the sanction of this decision. A conservative estimate is that fifty thousand people were sterilized in the United States by this authority. This legal precedent was ultimately used by the Nazis. In 1933, the statute enacted by Virginia under which Carrie Buck was sterilized became law in Germany.

The Nazi law was implemented swiftly. By the end of the first year that it was in effect, over fifty-six thousand people had been found to be defective and were sterilized. It is estimated that between 1933 and 1945, two million people were sterilized under the German law. In *Mein Kampf* (1927/1971), Hitler, discussing eugenics, argued that "the right of personal freedom recedes before the duty to preserve the race. The demand that defective people be prevented from propagating equally defective offspring is a demand of the clearest reason and if systematically executed represents the most humane act of mankind" (p. 255).

Eugenicists believed that human characteristics could be linked directly to individual genes. They held that not only physical traits like eye color and height but also personality attributes were determined by a single gene. Belief in genetic determination was extended to occupational preferences, academic interests, talents, and even character strengths and weaknesses. Such simplistic views about human beings were inherent in the conviction that sterilization would help stem a feared flood of incompetence resulting from a genetic blight, and such views were used to stereotype whole classes of people.

It was on the basis of these beliefs and this reasoning that Carrie Buck was sterilized. As described in several sources, however, the eugenic evidence in Carrie's case was inaccurate. Carrie's child, alleged to represent the "third generation of imbeciles," actually grew to be an honor roll student. After her sterilization, Carrie Buck was paroled to a village, where she later married the deputy sheriff. She lived a modest but productive and respectable life. Friends and employers attested to the fact that Carrie Buck was a competent and caring person. Indeed, mental health professionals who observed her late in her life found no evidence of mental retardation. If the eugenics researchers in her case had looked just two more branchings back on Carrie Buck's family tree, they would have discovered that her grandfather and great-grandfather in the Buck line were both prosperous farmers. Analysis of another branching back would have revealed the ironic likelihood that she was descended from "one of the most prominent families in Virginia's history."

Carrie Buck's story is a tragic saga of an injured life, as well as an important illustration of the allure and dangers of accepting simple answers to complex human questions. The lawyers, physicians, scientists, and politicians involved with the case were not sinister figures. They were convinced that they were serving the best interests of society by their actions. They advanced a scientific and political agenda that they felt would lead to the eradication of social problems and the prevention of suffering. They were wrong.

EUGENICS: A CONTINUING LEGACY

Support for the eugenics movement declined abruptly after the Second World War, particularly as the horrors of the Nazi's Race Hygiene Program became known. Shock at the realities of what had been done in the name of science and medicine diminished the amount of open rhetoric concerning superior and inferior groups of people. Eugenics, however, has taken many forms and continues to influence attitudes and behavior toward people who are perceived to be nonproductive or defective. A 1972 survey of obstetricians found that 97% favored sterilization of welfare mothers with illegitimate children. Paul Ramsay, a theologian at Princeton University, has said that, "the freedom of parenthood is not a license to produce seriously defective individuals" (Rodriguez-Tiras, 1982, p. 80). The Chicago Bar Association has recommended that the state of Illinois require premarital tests for "diseases or abnormalities causing birth defects" of people who apply for marriage licenses.

In discussions of the provision of life-sustaining treatment to newborns with mental retardation, a common issue has been projected quality of life. Advocates of the so-called quality of life position argue that decisions concerning euthanasia should be based on the prospective enjoyment and meaning the child is likely to derive from life. This, they contend, must be weighed against the suffering this individual is expected to experience and the degree to which he or she will be a burden to the family and society. From this perspective, human life is defined by factors of "fitness" to live.

Fletcher (1974, 1979) wrote much on the issue of quality of life. He defined *humanhood* as meeting minimal criteria, including an IQ higher than 20, the capacity to relate to people, a concern for others, and control of one's existence. If these criteria were strictly and narrowly applied to many of the children with mental retardation being served today in special education programs, these children would not be considered human. Their deficits in adaptive and cognitive skills would interfere with their performance in some or all of these areas, which would result in their being viewed as something less than human. Fletcher pointedly contended that any individual with Down syndrome, for example, is not a person. Not only children with mental retardation but significant numbers of children from other categories of disability would fall short of meeting these criteria. If all of the qualities and abilities Fletcher delineated must be manifested by the time an individual reaches maturity in order for him or her to be defined as possessing quality of life, many seemingly well-functioning adults would fail to qualify as human beings.

Erik Erikson has attributed inhumane judgments and actions by otherwise decent human beings to what he terms *pseudospeciation.* This is how he referred to the process of an "in group" defining an "out group" and deciding that its members are less than human. When it is believed that a certain group is not really human, the normal standards of human conduct no longer apply to them. Therefore, they may be treated in ways that would be unacceptable in the normal course of human relationships (Smith, 1993).

Mensa and Mental Retardation

Another example of the persistence of eugenic thought is to be found in the publications of a special interest group of the Mensa Society. The Mensa Society has only one qualification for membership: Applicants must show evidence that they have an IQ in the top 2% of the population on an intelligence test. The original idea for the formation of Mensa came from a radio broadcast by the psychologist and eugenics advocate Cyril Burt in 1945. He suggested that it might be interesting to sample the opinions of exceptionally intelligent people in a manner similar to the way Gallup polls were conducted. Within a year, the Mensa organization was founded by two English lawyers.

In his 1966 introduction to a book on Mensa research, Victor Serebriakoff wrote that "if Mensa steadily develops along the lines . . . laid down, it can make a rich and continual contribution not only to the national welfare but also to the advancement both of civilized and under-developed countries, and (it is surely not too much to say) to the peace and progress of mankind" (p. 21).

Although the original mission of the group may have been to use the talents of its members to help solve the world's problems, there is no evidence that Mensa has developed strategies for addressing world hunger, attempted to reduce the threat the nuclear war, or pursued the possibilities for world peace in the years since its founding. *Time* has reported (Bellafonte, 1993) that, in fact, the purpose of the organization has "evolved into something quite different: to bring highly intelligent people together to help them get dates" (p. 18). Writing on behalf of the fifty-five thousand members of American Mensa, Lisa Trombetta (1992) also characterized it as "primarily a social organization" (p. 6). Although the organization may have been largely social from its beginnings, Burt's original conception of polling the membership of Mensa on critical issues was implemented at least once. In 1962, over eighteen hundred Mensa members in the United Kingdom responded to an opinion survey that included items on nuclear testing, capital punishment, welfare, and sexuality. Of particular interest here, however, are the responses of the members to the one item about eugenics. When asked their opinions on avoiding the burden of caring for unhealthy dependents, 47% of the respondents favored the legalized killing of "sufficiently unhealthy or sub-normal infants."

Mensa in the United States has included a number of special interest groups, many of which are apparently social subgroups of the organization. One such special interest group has focused on the issue of eugenics. In their book, *Dangerous Diagnostics*, Nelkin and Tancredi (1989) reported that within Mensa there is "a small organization, founded in 1982, called the Eugenics Special Interest Group, that tries to provide a communications network for all people committed to enhancing human genetic quality; to develop sound, innovative projects to produce eugenic benefit; and to enlighten the public about the unique potential of eugenics with the intention of ultimately influencing public policy" (p. 13).

After corresponding with Mensa and eventually with the Eugenics Special Interest Group in 1991, I was able to obtain back issues of the Eugenics Special Interest Group publications and a place on the mailing list for subsequent issues. In his letter of confirmation of the subscription, the coordinator of the Eugenics Special Interest Group explained that the newest issue would soon be sent. He added the comment that "although our group is small, we believe that we have the potential to do a great deal of good for the whole human race." The April 1991 issue of the Eugenics Special Interest Group *Bulletin* contains several references to people called New Perfectionists who, through their eugenic actions and examples, will set the pattern for a brighter future. The use of the term *perfectionists* is a reference to the 19th century Oneida utopians and the religious and familial experiments conducted by John Noyes in his attempt to create a socially perfect community. The New Perfectionists are described as those who will now create an improved future through careful mating and selective reproduction. This issue of the *Bulletin* also contains a discussion of Down syndrome and culminates in several recommendations:

- It recommends routine amniocentesis for all pregnancies and termination of all Down syndrome pregnancies
- It encourages the development and use of earlier and improved tests for Down syndrome
- It argues at some length that no person with Down syndrome should be allowed to have children

At the end of this discussion, a ballot is provided and readers are invited to vote on the recommendations.

A review of back issues of the *Bulletin* yielded several interesting indications of the goals of the organization. The first issue, in 1982, provides an insight on the classic eugenic argument posited by the Eugenics Special Interest Group:

> Although the original idea dates back to antiquity, contemporary eugenics is a new frontier, drawing from such diverse disciplines as genetics, psychology, ethics and demography. It has profound consequences for the future of our species. If current dysgenic reproduction continues, it will eventually precipitate a protracted decline and deterioration of our society, while a reversal of the present trend could bring about an unprecedented cultural florescence.
>
> The Eugenics SIG [Special Interest Group] is a small beginning. But one must begin somewhere. We invite you to join in what we hope will be an exciting excursion. (p. 5)

The issues of the *Bulletin* that followed included an interview with Robert Graham, founder of the Repository for Germinal Choice, the sperm bank noted for its recruitment of deposits from William Shockley and other Nobel laureates, and an article by Arthur Jensen entitled "The Limited Plasticity of Human Intelligence." There was also an interview with Carl Bejema, a biologist who has been a prolific supporter of eugenic intervention for a number of years.

In 1984, the *Bulletin* published a letter from Robert Graham, who was also a member of the advisory board. It included comments of high praise for the publication:

> I do believe that the *Eugenics Bulletin* of the Eugenics Special Interest Group is now the outstanding eugenics publication in the country. The fall issue, with the Jensen article and the Bajema interview, was a milestone. (p. 10)

These comments stand in somewhat striking contradiction to what Graham was quoted a few years earlier as saying about the Mensa organization as a whole. In 1980, *Playboy* published an interview with William Shockley, the Nobel recipient for his work in the development of the transistor (Jones, 1980). Shockley was also an outspoken proponent of the existence of genetic differences in intelligence among racial and social groups. During the interview with *Playboy*, Shockley made remarks about Graham's attempts to recruit superior women to be the recipients of the Nobel Laureate sperm donations:

> Graham has been advertising for women in a publication sponsored by the Mensa Society. Mensa is a group of individuals who all have I.Q.s in the top 2 percent. But neither Graham nor I regard the Mensa population as being an ideal group. We both have the notion that, by and large, Mensa members have nothing going for them to speak of aside from a high performance on I.Q. tests. (p. 72)

My attempts to contact the Eugenics Special Interest Group since 1992 have been unsuccessful. I have searched for, but not found, subsequent issues of the *Bulletin*. If the subject were not so very serious, Mensa's excursion into eugenics might be considered simply uninformed or even ludicrous. The history of such excursions, however, has yielded consistently tragic results.

THE HUMAN GENOME PROJECT AND MENTAL RETARDATION

The identification of human genes is accelerating at a rate that not even molecular scientists would have predicted a few years ago. The center of this activity is the Human Genome Project. This coordinated effort is being compared to what the Manhattan Project meant for the development of the atomic bomb and to the effort of the Apollo Project, which led to the successful landing of human beings on the moon. The Human Genome Project has as its goal mapping and DNA sequencing, as quickly as possible, all of the estimated human genes. The word *genome* refers to the total genetic endowment contained on the chromosomes in every human cell. It now appears that the entire genome will be mapped and sequenced in the next few years.

With a genetic map so close in sight, scientists, and ethicists have initiated discussion of the ethical implications of the ability to identify prenatally, or even before conception, individuals or potential conceptions with genetically caused illnesses, disabilities, or weaknesses. Even conditions that emerge at middle age or later will be diagnosable before conception or during early fetal development. This creates questions about the ethics of controlling in ever more pervasive ways the characteristics and qualities of people who are allowed to be born. It also has profound implications for people who carry the potential for genetic disease, which will be detectable through genetic screening. People identified as having certain genetic weaknesses might, for example, be discriminated against by employers and by insurance companies.

The implications of the Human Genome Project for the field of disability are obviously enormous. It is possible that in a very few years the medical capacity for preventing all genetic forms of disability will be a reality. Is there a right to life for individuals with disabilities in this context? Will parents who may carry the genes for disabilities have the right of reproduction taken from them either explicitly or through coercion? Are disabilities always diseases to be prevented or are they human conditions worthy of being valued? Conversations on these questions have begun but must become more common and active in the field.

MENTAL RETARDATION, "FELT NECESSITIES," AND ETHICS

In 1881, Oliver Wendell Holmes published a book titled *The Common Law*. On the first page, he wrote:

> The life of the law has not been logic; it has been experience. The felt necessities of the time, the prevalent moral and political theories, intuitions of public policy, avowed or unconscious, even the prejudices which judges share with their fellow-men [are the sources of law].

The Human Genome Project will most certainly result in scientific knowledge and medical capabilities that will bring into question the issue of "felt necessities" in relation to fundamental values and disabilities. The technology of tubal ligation and vasectomy was developed in the 1890s; by 1927, it was a "felt necessity" of society that those deemed defective, according to eugenic pseudoscience, must be sterilized. The Human Genome Project will provide insights into human nature with a scientific validity incomparable to the inaccuracies of the eugenics movement. It will provide for the development of technologies that will eclipse anything that medicine has known before. The potentials for human benefit are obviously enormous. It seems to me, however, that the greatest challenge posed by the Human Genome Project will be to conduct its work and provide the benefits of its efforts to a world of people who are seen as much more than the sum total of their biological components. To rise above the temptations and dangers of biological determinism, we must continue to see people as agents of freedom and dignity.

As advocates for people with disabilities, our first commitment must be to basic human rights and values—even when expedient intervention in the lives of people with mental retardation seems to be what is best for them and society, and even when the "felt necessities of our times" seem to urge so compellingly for society to act quickly and efficiently. The ethical foundations of human life are to be found in human sources. The early eugenicists looked to evolutionary theory and Mendelian genetics for moral truths. They felt that natural selection and Mendelian gene distributions could provide models for social ethics. The failure of this approach was evidenced in the needless institutionalization of those deemed to be "unfit" for the social "struggle," in the sterilization of people inaccurately assessed to be the carriers of defective genes, and in the moral horrors of the Holocaust.

Moral and ethical agency is an attribute of people, not of medicine or the scientific method. The recognition that we are ethical and moral agents and that the decisions of what we should do, as opposed to what we can do, rests with us as people is intimidating. On the other hand, it is exciting. As the power of science to benefit humanity grows through the work of the Human Genome Project, so grows the importance of ethical questions about the use and the yield of that power in the lives of people with disabilities. The great challenge of this decade may be to ensure that there are exchanges between people who are motivated by making scientific and medical discoveries and those who seek to understand the human truth of those discoveries for the lives or people with the differences we call disabilities.

REFERENCES AND FURTHER READINGS

Bellafonte, G. (1993). Hey Einstein, let's jacuzzi. *Time, 42*(3), 18.
Bishop, J., & Waldholz, M. (1990). *Genome*. New York: Simon & Schuster.

Bulletin. (1982). Eugenics Special Interest Group, Brooklyn, NY.

Bulletin. (1984). Eugenics Special Interest Group, Brooklyn, NY.

Bulletin. (1991). Eugenics Special Interest Group, Nassau, NY.

Fletcher, J. (1974). Four indicators of humanhood: The inquiry matures. *The Hastings Center Report, 4,* 4–7.

Fletcher, J. (1979). *Humanhood: Essays in biomedical ethics.* Buffalo, NY: Prometheus.

Gould, S. (1984). Carrie Buck's daughter. *Natural History, 93*(7), 14–18.

Hitler, A. (1971). *Mein kampf.* Boston: Houghton Mifflin. (Original English translation published 1927)

Holmes, O. W. (1881). *The common law.* Boston: Little, Brown.

Hubbard, R., & Wald, E. (1993). *Exploding the gene myth.* Boston: Beacon.

Hughes, T. (1973). *Mensa: A study of high intelligence.* Memphis, TN: Memphis State University Press.

Jones, S. (1980). Interview with William Shockley. *Playboy, 27,* 69–102.

Nelkin, D., & Tancredi, L. (1989). *Dangerous diagnostics: The social power of biological information.* New York: Basic Books.

Rodriguez-Trias, H. (1982). Sterilization abuse. In R. Hubbard & E. Wald (Eds.), *Biological woman: The convenient myth.* Cambridge, MA: Schenkemen.

Serebriakoff, V. (1966). *IQ: A Mensa analysis and history.* London: Hutchinson of London.

Smith, J. D. (1993). *The Eugenic assault on America: Scenes in red, white, and black.* Fairfax, VA: George Mason University Press.

Smith, J. D., & Nelson, K. R. (1989). *The sterilization of Carrie Buck.* Far Hills, NJ: New Horizon.

Thomas, R. B. (1977). *The man who would be perfect.* Philadelphia: University of Pennsylvania Press.

Trombetta, L. (1992). No nerds please. *The New Republic, 203*(7), 6.

9

Eugenics Revisited

Buck Versus Bell *and* The Bell Curve

Otto Hofmann, a high-ranking SS officer, was one of the facilitators of policies aimed at what the Nazis conceptualized as "the final solution to the Jewish question." He was head of the Race and Settlement Main Office of the Reichsfuehrer-SS. The fifth volume of *Trials of the War Criminals Before the Nuremberg Military Tribunals* (1950) contains records of Hofmann's conviction for war crimes. It states that evidence establishes beyond any reasonable doubt Hofmann's guilt and his criminal responsibility for the following criminal activities:

> forcible abortions on Eastern workers; taking away infants of Eastern workers; the illegal and unjust punishment of foreign nationals for sexual intercourse with Germans; [and] hampering the reproduction of foreign populations [i.e., forced sterilizations]. (p. 160)

The fifth volume of records of the *Nuremberg Tribunals* contains the accounts of the conviction of Otto Hofmann; the fourth volume includes documents that were entered in his defense. Among them is an abstract prepared in 1937 by the Information Service of the Racial-Political Office of the Reich Administration. It concerns what are called "Race Protection Laws of Other Countries" and appears to have been entered as evidence on Hofmann's behalf to show that the practices he engaged in during the war were based on precedents from other "civilized" nations. It contains a litany of sterilization policies from countries such as Denmark, Finland, Norway, and Sweden. The list ends with a detailed discussion of sterilization laws in the United States. It references the Supreme Court decision in *Buck v. Bell*:

> Those affected by the law were primarily criminals, feeble-minded, insane, epileptics, alcoholics and narcotic addicts, as well as prostitutes. Although almost all states try to carry out sterilization on a voluntary basis, the courts have more than once ordered compulsory sterilizations. In a judgment of the Supreme Court of [1927] . . . it says, among other things, "It is better for everybody if society, instead of waiting until it has to execute degenerate offspring or leave them to starve because of feeblemindedness, can prevent obviously inferior individuals from propagating their own kind. The principle justifying compulsory vaccination is broad enough to cover the severing of the Fallopian tubes."(p. 1159)

Reading Justice Oliver Wendell Holmes's majority opinion in *Buck v. Bell* is a sobering reminder of the credibility that was bestowed upon eugenic philosophy and policy, and of the atrocities that were committed under the guise of science. The now-famous phrase he used sums up the prevailing feelings of that time: "Three generations of imbeciles are enough." His reasoning and language are consistent with the eugenic view of the time that many socially undesirable traits, including mental retardation, are largely hereditary.

Inherent in this view is the idea that even complex human traits can be traced to simple genetic causes. Eugenicists believed, in fact, that most human characteristics would be linked directly to single genes. They held that not only physical traits, like eye color and height, but also intelligence and personality attributes are determined by isolated genes. This confidence in Mendelian genetics was extended to the determination of occupational preferences, academic interests, talents, and even character strengths and weaknesses. Eugenicists at that time claimed that mechanical skill, artistic talent, and musical ability were recessive gene traits. Shiftlessness was also included in this list of recessively determined character traits. Violent temperament, it was reasoned, must be a dominant gene trait because it does not skip generations. A study titled *The Nam Family: A Study in Cacogenics* reported that laziness is a dominant trait, whereas abusive drinking and shyness are simple recessives (Estabrook & Davenport, 1912).

These enthusiastic excursions into biological determinism and reductionism may sound humorous when viewed from our current perspective, but they were the basis for great human tragedy. Such reductionistic views about human beings were inherent in the conviction that eugenics would stem a flood of incompetence resulting from genetic blight.

Although the eugenics movement was obsessed with race and ethnicity, its proponents also focused on perceived differences in social and economic classes. In her 1988 book, *White Trash: The Eugenic Family Studies*, Nicole Hahn Rafter portrayed the family degeneracy studies that were conducted as part of the eugenics movement as having been focused primarily on lower-class Caucasian families, on the "poor white trash" of early twentieth-century America. When Carrie Buck's sterilization case was first heard, a report was submitted to the lower court as testimony by Laughlin, the author of the model that Virginia had adopted for its sterilization law. He analyzed information on Carrie Buck and her family. In commenting on her heritage, Laughlin said, "These people belong to the shiftless, ignorant and worthless class of anti-social whites of the South . . . [they are an] ignorant and moving class of people (p. 14)."

Goddard, in his famous 1912 book on the Kallikak family, made the following comments about the lower-socioeconomic-class people who were the subjects of his study:

> If all of the slum districts of our cities were removed tomorrow and model tenements built in their places, we would still have slums in a week's time because we have these mentally defective people who can never be taught to live otherwise than as they have been living. Not until we take care of this class and see to it that their lives are guided by intelligent people, shall we remove these sores from our social life. (pp. 70–71)

Contrary to these comments, my visit to the Kallikak family, which I described in my 1985 book *Minds Made Feeble*, revealed that there were not discrete "good" and "bad" bloodlines in the family. Rather, Goddard's perception was colored by what he was looking for in these families. He wanted support for his argument about the social threat posed by what he perceived to be a class of genetically inferior people. He made the characters fit the story he wanted to tell.

It was on the basis of these beliefs and this reasoning, however, that Carrie Buck was sterilized. Thus, the precedent was established for the suspension of the rights of some individuals and classes for the protection of society. These views, with the credibility afforded by what was accepted as scientific fact, became powerful forces in shaping public opinion and social policy.

The impact of eugenics was always greatest on those who were the poorest, least educated, and least powerful in society. Their lives were seen as problems for social control. Their protection and their rights were subjugated to what was considered compelling scientific evidence.

In *The Bell Curve* (1994), the authors, Richard Herrnstein and Charles Murray, succeeded in bringing the attention of the public back to issues of ethnicity, social class, and intelligence. Although I suspect that there were relatively few people who actually read the 847-page book, it stimulated much controversy and comment in the media. In fact, the book presented little that was new in terms of data and much that was old in terms of reductionism. The arguments the authors advanced essentially laid the responsibility for poverty and discrimination at the doorsteps of the victims. It called for the abandonment of hope, opportunity, and dignity for millions of people. It was filled with classic eugenic principles, veiled, only thinly, by a new cover. Eugenics, old and new, deserves the scrutiny and critique of those in the field of disabilities who recognize all too well its disturbing and divisive messages.

REFERENCES AND FURTHER READINGS

Buck v. Bell. (1927). 274 U.S. 200, 47 S. Cr. 584.

Buck v. Priddy. (1924). Amherst County Clerk of Courts Office, Amherst County Courthouse: Amherst, Virginia.

Estabrook, A. H., & Davenport, C. (1912). *The Nam family: A study in cacogenics.* Cold Harbor, NY: Eugenics Records Office.

Goddard, H. H. (1912). *The Kallikak family: A study in the heredity of feeble-mindedness,* New York: Macmillan.

Herrnstein, R., & Murray, C. (1994). *The bell curve: Intelligence and class structure in American life.* New York: The Free Press.

Laughlin, H. H. (1929). *The legal status of eugenical sterilization.* Chicago: Psychopathic Laboratory of the Municipal Court of Chicago.

Rafter, N. H. (1988). *White trash: The eugenic family studies 1877–1919.* Boston: Northeastern University Press.

Smith, J. D. (1985). *Minds made feeble: The myth and legacy of the Kallikaks.* Rockville, MD: Aspen.

Trials of war criminals before the Nuremberg military tribunals (Vols. 4 & 5). (1950). Washington, DC: U.S. Government Printing Office.

10

Old Texts, Disabilities, and the Persistent Argument

For Whom the Bell Curves

I recently surveyed secondary and college biology textbooks published in the United States during the first half of the twentieth century. I did this in an attempt to comprehend the impact of the eugenics movement during that period on the ways that biology and health literacy were taught in schools and colleges. I found that most textbooks of that era reported the arguments of the eugenicists as if they were established and undisputed scientific facts. The studies of the Jukes, the Kallikaks, Carrie Buck, and other family pedigree studies were presented as compelling evidence for simple genetic transmission of complex intellectual and personality attributes.

The textbook that I found of greatest interest was first published in 1914: G. W. Hunter's *A Civic Biology*. It may, in fact, be the most infamous textbook in the history of the teaching of biology. It was the text that John Scopes used in his high school class in Dayton, Tennessee, and it became the major piece of evidence in what is often called the "Monkey Trial" of 1925, in which Scopes was tried for teaching Darwin's theory of evolution in a public school.

In *A Civic Biology,* Hunter presented an illustration of the evolutionary tree and placed human beings in "the group of mammals which includes the monkeys, apes and man, we call primates." John Scopes's use of this part of the textbook in teaching his students was central to Tennessee's case against him for teaching evolution.

It is important to note that although the brief mention of evolution included in the text was central to one of the most famous court cases in history concerning science education, other information presented in the book was not considered controversial. The page following the introduction of evolutionary theory, for example, includes the following observations:

> **The Races of Man.** At the present time there exist upon the earth five races or varieties of man, each very different from the other in instincts, social customs, and to an extent, in structure. These are the Ethiopian or Negro type, originating in Africa; the Malay or brown race, from the islands of the Pacific; the American Indian; the Mongolian or yellow race, including the natives of China, Japan, and the Eskimos; and finally, the highest type of all, the Caucasians, represented by the civilized white inhabitants of Europe and America. (p. 196)

Although encountering this stark presentation of social Darwinism in a textbook that was condemned for its discussion of evolution is fascinating, of even greater interest to me is a discussion later in the text about eugenics. The author cautioned students to select a mate who is free of genetic diseases. This warning was furthered by assertions that conditions such as tuberculosis and mental retardation must be eliminated by eugenic measures. Hunter included several pages of descriptions of eugenic family pedigree studies to support the validity of these efforts.

I find it ironic that evolution as presented in *A Civic Biology* became a central issue in public education, whereas eugenics as portrayed in the same book is a concept that is still only dimly understood by many teachers and their students. Stephen Jay Gould (1989) made the following observation in his foreword to my book *The Sterilization of Carrie Buck.*

> Eugenical sterilization surely had a greater impact on people's lives than creationism. . . . Yet while books, not to mention television dramas, abound about the Scopes trial, no one has yet properly presented Carrie's story to a mass audience. (p. xv)

In his biographical profile of John Scopes, J. R. Tompkins (1965) said that *A Civic Biology*

> commended the Darwinian theory of the origin of species with nonchalant candor. Scopes did not question this position for it

seemed like standard fare for modern high school biology; after all, this was precisely what he had been taught in high school and college. (p. 11)

It is likely that Scopes had also been taught the concept of a racial hierarchy and of the necessity of eugenic control of human traits. It is obvious that these ideas were not questioned even in the glare of public attention that the Scopes trial brought to the textbook that presented them as facts.

Lately I have been thinking much about the influence of another book, *The Bell Curve* by Richard Herrnstein and Charles Murray. Although Murray has disclaimed that he and the late Herrnstein were advancing eugenic arguments, the echoes of very old rhetoric are in its pages. When I read it, I was reminded of another of the old textbooks that I reviewed. In 1922, Burlingame, Heath, Martin, and Pierce made the following observations in their book *General Biology:*

> Probably not more than 10 or 15 percent of American Negroes equal or exceed in intelligence of the average White. The intelligence of the average Negro is vastly inferior to that of the average White, and the mulatto occupies a position about mid-way between. . . . The immigrants who have been coming to us from the extreme southern and southeastern parts of Europe (South Italians, Portuguese, Greeks and Slavs) are in general distinctly inferior to those who come to us from Northern, Central, and Western Europe. The influx of the former has been so great, and their rate of reproduction is so excessive, as to give rise to a serious menace. . . . No nation can afford to overlook the danger that the average quality of its germ plasm may gradually deteriorate as a result of unrestricted immigration. (pp. 526–527)

Seventy-two years later, the works of Herrnstein and Murray sounded disturbingly familiar:

> The difference in test scores between African-Americans and European-Americans as measured in dozens of reputable studies has converged on approximately a one standard of deviation difference for several decades. Translated into centiles, this means that the average white person tests higher than about 84 percent of the population of the blacks and that the average black person tests higher than about 16 percent of the population of whites. (p. 269)

> The rules that currently govern immigration provide the other major source of dysgenic pressure. It appears that the mean IQ of immigrants in the 1980s works out to about 95. The low IQ may not be a problem; in the past, immigrants have sometimes shown large

increases on such measures. But other evidence indicates that the self-selection process that used to attract the classic American immigrant—brave, hard-working, imaginative, self-starting, and often of high IQ—has been changing, and with it the nature of some of the immigrant population. (p. 341)

Putting the pieces together, something worth worrying about is happening to the cognitive capital of the country. Improved health, education, and childhood interventions may hide the demographic effects, but that does not reduce their importance. Whatever good things we can accomplish with changes in the environment would be that much more effective if they did not have to fight a demographic head wind. (p. 342)

Herrnstein and Murray wrapped themselves in the mantle of science and claimed that what they reported, although it may not be popularly accepted, is scientific fact that must be faced. They introduced their presentation of this data with the following conclusive statements about intelligence and intelligence testing, which they described as "beyond significant technical dispute":

1. There is such a thing as a general factor of cognitive ability on which human beings differ

2. All standardized tests of academic aptitude or achievement measure this general factor to some degree, but IQ tests expressly designed for that purpose measure it most accurately

3. IQ scores match, to a first degree, whatever it is that people mean when they use the word *intelligent* or *smart* in ordinary language

4. IQ scores are stable, although not perfectly so, over much of a person's life

5. Properly administered IQ tests are not demonstrably biased against social, economic, ethnic, or racial groups

6. Cognitive ability is substantially heritable, apparently no less than 40 percent and no more than 80 percent (pp. 23–24)

Herrnstein and Murray explained that when they use the term "beyond significant technical dispute" they mean that if there were a gathering of "top experts on testing and cognitive ability, drawn from all points of view, to argue over these points, away from the television cameras and reporters, it would quickly become apparent that a consensus already exists on all of the points, in some cases amounting to near unanimity" (p. 23).

I was left stunned by this comment. Surely there are no more contentious and persistent questions in the social sciences than those surrounding the nature of intelligence and its measurement. It is appalling that Herrnstein and Murray would make the claim that their answers to these questions are "beyond significant technical dispute." It is frightening that the perceived authority of their claim may convince many that it is accurate.

The greatest challenge created by *The Bell Curve* for scholars and practitioners in the field of disabilities is to voice our comprehension of the complex nature of human intelligence and its meaning in the lives of individuals. It is also imperative that we help others understand the danger of proposing simple solutions to complex personal and social questions.

Mental retardation is hardly mentioned in *The Bell Curve*. When it is discussed, it is seen only as a problem, as pathology. The right of people to be valued for their variety, their unpredictability, and the unexpectedness in their lives goes completely unrecognized.

I hope that if the textbooks of the early twenty-first century are surveyed someday, mental retardation and other disabilities will be presented as catalysts that increased the awareness of the critical choices that only individuals and families can make about the character and direction of their lives. I believe that during the next few years the decision will be made about whether disabilities will be viewed as a collection of diseases and deficits to be cured and prevented or as complex features of human diversity, features to be better understood as a part of the human diversity we celebrate.

REFERENCES AND FURTHER READINGS

Burlingame, L., Heath, H., Martin, E., & Pierce, G. (1922). *General biology.* New York: Henry Holt.

Gould, S. J. (1989). Foreword. In J. D. Smith & K. R. Nelson, *The sterilization of Carrie Buck.* Far Hills, NJ: New Horizon.

Herrnstein, R., & Murray, C. (1994). *The bell curve: Intelligence and class structure in American life.* New York: The Free Press.

Hunter, G. W. (1914). *A civic biology: Presented in problems.* New York: American Book Company.

Smith, J. D., & Nelson, K. R. (1989). *The sterilization of Carrie Buck.* Far Hills, NJ: New Horizon.

Tompkins, J. R. (1965). *D-days at Dayton.* Baton Rouge: Louisiana State University Press.

11

Different Voices of Advocacy

Helen Keller and Burton Blatt

In his 1995 book *Inventing the Feeble Mind*, James Trent described mental retardation as a

> construction whose changing meaning is shaped both by individuals who initiate and administer policies, programs and practices, and by the social context to which these individuals are responding. (p. 2)

Trent argued that the meaning of *disabilities* has been constructed sometimes in the name of science, sometimes in the name of caring for people with disabilities, and sometimes in the name of social or economic necessity. Each of these reasons for describing people with disabilities, however, has also been used for the purpose of controlling these people because they are perceived to be a threat or an inconvenience to society. The construction of the meaning of *disability* has, from this perspective, been motivated more by a search for control than by a concern for the best interests of people with disabilities.

HELEN KELLER: A MAGNIFICENT EXCEPTION

There have been, of course, exceptions to prevalent social constructions of the meaning of *disabilities.* These exceptions have most often occurred when an individual with a disability achieved prominence, and visibility, through extraordinary accomplishments. Helen Keller is an outstanding example of a person with severe disabilities but magnificent achievements who was, therefore, able to eclipse the prevailing attitudes about people with those disabilities. Her life and her relationship with her teacher Annie Sullivan are inspiring and worthy of study. In his biography of Helen Keller, Joseph Lash (1980) observed that her disabilities may have been necessary vehicles for the achievement of her extraordinary insight and influence. He quoted one of her contemporaries as having speculated on what she might have accomplished if she had not been blind and deaf, and then added that perhaps these were the differences that created her "high intelligence and purity of soul." Helen Keller agreed, saying, "I have made my limitations tools of learning and true joy."

Some years ago, while working on a research project in the Manuscript Division of the Library of Congress, I happened upon a reference to letters from and to Helen Keller in the Alexander Graham Bell Collection. As I looked through these papers, I became enthralled with them. Here were letters written by Helen Keller, Annie Sullivan, Alexander Graham Bell, and others that presented a unique and important view of Helen, her friendships, and her philosophy.

On July 5, 1918, Helen Keller wrote a letter to Alexander Graham Bell about the fingerspelling method of her teacher, Annie Sullivan, that I think portrays why she always called her "Teacher," as well as the epiphany that Annie Sullivan created in her student's life. Helen Keller described the moment when she understood that the fingerspelling that she felt in her hand had meaning.

> Sometimes I feel that in that supreme moment she thought me into being. . . . My fingers still glow with the feel of the first word that opened its golden heart to me. How everything seemed to think, to live! Shall I, in all the years of eternity, forget the torrent of wonders that rushed upon me out of the darkness and silence?

I soon shared these letters with my wonderful colleague Burton Blatt, who served as a mentor to so many of my generation. Burt read the letters, just as he approached most things, with vigor, insight, and depth of feeling. We discussed his using the letters in a manuscript, and I encouraged him to do so. He subsequently cited some of the letters in an article that was published shortly after his death.

In that article, Blatt (1985) quoted extensively from several of the letters. He prefaced these excerpts by explaining that he chose them primarily to draw lessons from these glimpses into the relationship between Helen Keller and her beloved teacher Annie Sullivan.

HELEN KELLER AND THE
PARAMETERS OF ADVOCACY

Blatt (1985) referred to the breadth of Helen Keller's advocacy for the rights of many of the world's most troubled people. She became a political activist and spokesperson for the victims of poverty, economic exploitation, gender bias, and other forms of oppression. He described Helen Keller's advocacy as follows:

> As she strove to free herself from the difficulties which disease created in her, she more and more sought to understand the difficulties which society created for mankind's downtrodden multitudes. (p. 409)

Burton Blatt had a keen sense of history. He understood that the facts and personalities of any historical period are intimately entwined with the social and philosophical context of that period. He also understood that a seemingly clear "good guy–bad guy" dichotomy in the study of any historical topic is likely to be incorrect. He understood that "real" history is fraught with contradictions and disappointments. He knew that this was particularly true of the study of the history of mental retardation.

My own sense of the contradictory nature of the study of the history of mental retardation was challenged recently as I was reading a fascinating 1980 book titled *The Black Stork*. The author, Martin Pernick, provided an interesting account of a controversy that began in 1915 and that surrounded the work of a physician who openly practiced euthanasia on "defective" newborns. Dr. Harry Haiselden not only allowed infants with severe disabilities to die, but he administered drugs to speed the death of several of these newborns. He also campaigned for the widespread adoption of these practices and produced and starred in a movie promoting euthanasia, *The Black Stork*. The film was based on Haiselden's eugenic arguments and was shown in commercial movie theaters from 1916 through the 1920s.

In reading about this controversy, I was intrigued by a reference the author made to Helen Keller's support of Haiselden's eugenic campaign. When I reviewed her position on the euthanasia of infants with mental retardation, my perception of the contradictory nature of historical realities, and my sense of Helen Keller as a person of her time, was deepened.

In her statement, Helen Keller expressed the following opinions:

> It is the possibilities of happiness, intelligence and power that give life its sanctity, and they are absent in the case of a poor, misshapen,

paralyzed, unthinking creature. . . . The toleration of such anomalies tends to lessen the sacredness in which normal life is held.

It seems to me that the simplest, wisest thing to do would be to submit cases like that of the malformed idiot baby to a jury of expert physicians. . . . A mental defective . . . is almost sure to be a potential criminal. The evidence before a jury of physicians considering the case of an idiot would be exact and scientific. Their findings would be free from the prejudice and inaccuracy of untrained observation. They would act only in case of true idiocy, where there could be no hope of mental development. (cited in Pernick, 1980, pp. 173–174)

Contradictions and "Good" History

Considering the history of mental retardation, Burton Blatt (1987) wrote that

virtually all histories in our field are dangerously incomplete. . . . That which is preserved may be less relevant than that which is unknown; and the 'facts,' however pertinent, are to a degree divorced from the social-psychological context of the period. . . . To understand what actually occurred (and why) requires one to know what the times were like. (p. 17)

Helen Keller's development as an intellectual and as an advocate took place within the context of the scientific and social movement of eugenics. It also occurred within the political and philosophical environment of progressivism. Progressive thought held that most of the problems of society and of individuals could and should be reduced to scientific terms and resolved by scientific means. Helen Keller's trust of a "jury" of physicians is very consistent with the faith in scientific progress that characterized the cultural climate of her formative years as a social activist. Her opinion that "true idiocy" lessens the sanctity of "normal life" reflects the eugenic principles to which she was certainly exposed. These arguments supported euthanasia, sterilization, and institutionalization. They asserted that these and other eugenic measures were in the best interests of both society and the "defective" individual.

Helen Keller's voice of advocacy was bold for its time. It was focused, however, on the potential for social intercourse and productivity in the lives of ignored, misunderstood, and exploited people. In that regard, she moved beyond a social context that devalued many people with blindness, deafness, and other physical disabilities, for example, and crusaded for their rights to earn a place in society. She was a courageous advocate for these people and she deserves the admiration embodied in Burton Blatt's (1985) tribute to her:

Seeing with her hands and her soul while others could see only with their eyes, she was led to the idea of a new social order, a world free of worker exploitation, free of preventable disease, free of sexism, free of all forms of human oppression. (p. 409)

BURTON BLATT'S ADVOCACY: THE GOLDEN RULE AND BEYOND

Burt Blatt's advocacy, like that of Helen Keller, was grounded in a commitment to human rights and human dignity. In his voice, however, rights were not couched in the expectation of productivity, and dignity was not contingent on independence. He urged that advocates work for others not as they would have others treat them but as they would treat themselves in the most challenging of circumstances.

His voice as an advocate is heard clearly in his description of the relationship between Helen Keller and Annie Sullivan. He believed that before Helen Keller was liberated to become a brilliant and famous person, she was a person with mental retardation. He felt that the fact that she functioned as a person with mental retardation is one of the two most central facets of the "miracle" of her life story. The second central facet of the story, according to Blatt, is that Annie Sullivan's commitment to being Helen Keller's Teacher was unconditional. When Sullivan boarded a train in Boston destined for Tuscumbia, Alabama, it was not with the expectation that Helen Keller would become a miracle student and she a miracle worker. In describing Annie Sullivan's commitment and advocacy, Blatt (1982) said:

Indeed, had Annie spent her entire life with Helen, and had Helen never made a single intelligible response, everything we know about Annie Sullivan suggests that she would not have felt that her life was wasted. (p. 137)

LEGACIES AND CHALLENGES

Through the memory of Helen Keller and Annie Sullivan, we are challenged to hold firm to a belief in the miracle of commitments that are unconditional and sustained. We are also reminded of the contradictions that characterize history and even the greatest of personalities.

Through Burt Blatt's mentorship, we are strengthened by a legacy of hopefulness. We are challenged to believe that the conquest of disabilities is possible.

REFERENCES AND FURTHER READINGS

Blatt, B. (1982). *In and out of the university: Essays on higher and special education.* Austin, TX: Pro-Ed.

Blatt, B. (1985). Friendly letters on the correspondence of Helen Keller, Anne Sullivan, and Alexander Graham Bell. *Exceptional Children, 51,* 405–409.

Blatt, B. (1987). *The conquest of mental retardation.* Austin, TX: Pro-Ed.

Foner, P. (1967). *Helen Keller: Her socialist years, writings and speeches.* New York: International.

Keller, H. (1918, July 5). Letter to Alexander Graham Bell. Alexander Graham Bell collection, Manuscript Division, Library of Congress, Washington, DC.

Lash, J. (1980). *Helen and teacher: The story of Helen Keller and Anne Sullivan Macy.* New York: Delacorte.

Pernick, M. (1980). *The black stork: Eugenics and the death of "defective" babies in American medicine and motion pictures since 1915.* New York: Oxford University Press.

Trent, J. (1995). *Inventing the feeble mind: A history of mental retardation in the United States.* Berkeley: University of California Press.

12

A Place or No Place for Disabilities

Disney's Tarzan, *Edgar Rice Burroughs's Eugenics, and Visions of Utopian Perfection*

One of the classic stories in the history of disabilities is that of Victor, a child whom seemingly grew up without human nurturance in the Caune Woods of southern France. "The Wild Boy of Aveyron" created great excitement when he was captured by hunters in 1799. He was examined by the eminent physician Phillipe Pinel and was diagnosed as being an incurable "idiot."

A younger physician, Jean Marc-Gaspard Itard, questioned Pinel's diagnosis and prognosis. He also asked for the opportunity to try to educate the boy he had named Victor. He was confident that he could bring the child out of his animalistic state of existence. Itard's request was granted.

Even though Victor made progress with many of the skills that Itard set out to teach him, the physician's optimism faded as he was unable to teach the boy to speak. After five years, in fact, Itard concluded that Victor would never learn spoken language. He discontinued his instruction completely and resigned himself to Pinel's earlier diagnosis. Victor's social and language disabilities were a function of "mental atrophy."

Even though Itard believed that he had failed with Victor, educators, psychologists and physicians have admired him for centuries. Many feel that his educational philosophy and instructional techniques mark the beginning of special education as a discipline. Itard has been given the accolade of the "Father of Special Education."

TARZAN AND THE TRIUMPH OF HEREDITY

The 1999 Disney animation of the story of Tarzan provides an interesting and provocative contrast to Itard's account of Victor's life. The hero of the film is deprived of human contact from infancy and is adopted by a family of apes. Amazingly, however, he thrives and becomes "King of the Jungle." More amazingly, he adapts rapidly when he first encounters other human beings. His social and language skills develop at a pace that enables him to prevail in human culture as successfully as he has in the jungle.

The Disney version of the Tarzan tale is pleasing and engaging. The human and animal characters are interesting and entertaining, and the heroes and villains are clearly discernable. Goodness and justice, of course, prevail at the film's conclusion.

The first of Edgar Rice Burroughs's Tarzan novels, *Tarzan of the Apes,* was published in 1912. The first Tarzan movie premiered in 1917. Many Tarzan sequels followed the original novel, and several generations of Hollywood Tarzans portrayed the hero. No human actor, however, could satisfy Burroughs's conception of how Tarzan should look and act. The author decided that animation was the most promising way to present his character. In a 1936 letter to his son, Burroughs wrote of his desire to form a company called Tarzantoons and to make an animated version of his story. He explained, "The cartoon must be good. It must approximate Disney excellence."

Unlike the early movie versions of his Tarzan story that were disappointing to Burroughs, the animation in the recent Disney movie would probably have been gratifying to him. It would be interesting to know if Burroughs would also have appreciated the significant changes in his story that were made for the Disney script. As with most Disney films, the overt message of the film is that the greedy and evil character of the villain is defeated by the virtue of the hero. The message of Burroughs's book is much more complex than this—both philosophically and politically. His infant Tarzan is raised by a family of apes and, as in the Disney movie, the child grows up stronger than his peers and conquers his environment. According to Burroughs's book, however, Tarzan thrives and becomes the "master" of his jungle community for one very compelling reason: Millions of years of evolution had prepared people of his race and class to do so. In 1930 Burroughs wrote:

I was mainly interested in playing with the idea of a contrast between heredity and environment. For this purpose I selected an infant child of a race strongly marked by hereditary characteristics of the finer and noble sort, and at an age where he could not have been influenced by associations with creatures of his own kind. I threw him into an environment as diametrically opposite that to which he had been born as I might well conceive. (pp. 29–30)

Burroughs was fascinated with eugenics. *Tarzan of the Apes* (1912) was not written for children. On the contrary, it was written as Burroughs's epic of eugenic triumph. He believed that human heredity had reached its zenith in British aristocracy. The story begins when mutinous sailors maroon Tarzan's English parents on the coast of Africa. Early in the novel, Burroughs describes the father, Lord Greystroke, as "the type of Englishman that one likes best to associate with the noblest monuments of historic achievement upon a thousand battlefields—a strong, virile man— mentally, morally, physically." Tarzan's mother, also of the English nobility, dies shortly after he is born, following an assault on her by a great ape. His father is killed when a group of apes return to the family's cabin. The male apes hear a cry from the crib and intend to destroy Tarzan as well, but they are persuaded to spare the infant by a female ape, Kala. She is in mourning over the death of her own child and, against the advice of the other apes, she adopts the human baby.

In his earliest developmental years, Tarzan lags behind the young apes in his group in climbing, running, and swinging through trees. Similar to the arguments that have been made about withholding care and treatment from infants with disabilities for eugenic reasons, Kala's husband urges that they abandon this clearly defective child.

"He will never be a great ape," he argued. "Always you will have to carry him and protect him. What good will he be to the tribe? None, only a burden. . . . Let us leave him quietly sleeping among the tall grasses, that you may bear other and stronger apes to guard us in our old age." "Never. . . . " replied Kala. "If I must carry him forever, so be it." (Burroughs, 1912, pp. 55–56)

Soon, however, Tarzan's physical development catches up with that of his ape peers, and by adolescence, he has surpassed them in physical prowess. He has become the young "king" of his environment. Even more remarkable, however, are his intellectual feats. His reasoning and problem- solving skills make him clearly superior to all of the other inhabitants of the jungle. Most astounding, Tarzan returns to the cabin home of his parents and discovers picture books, a primer, and a dictionary. Using these, he teaches himself to read and write. In describing the epiphany that reading gave Tarzan about himself, Burroughs (1912) wrote:

By the time he was seventeen, he had learned to read the simple, child's primer and had fully realized the true and wonderful purpose of the [letters in the books]. . . . No longer did he feel shame for his hairless body or his human features, for now his reason told him that he was of a different race from his wild and hairy companions. . . . From then on his progress was rapid. With the help of the great dictionary and the active intelligence of a healthy mind endowed by inheritance with more than ordinary reasoning powers he shrewdly guessed at much he could not really understand. (p. 83)

Soon Tarzan becomes aware of the presence of other humans in the jungle. He observes a group of African warriors and studies their skin color and other physical features. Burroughs describes in detail Tarzan's thoughts about what he perceives to be humanlike, but not fully human, creatures. He also provides an account of the thoughts and feelings Tarzan expresses when he kills one of these warriors, a sense of relatedness to but distance from this "other kind" of man.

The Disney animation avoids the race issue by removing all African men and women from the story. When other Europeans arrive on the shore of Tarzan's home, he and the animals are the only inhabitants. In Burroughs's (1912) book, however, race is a dominant theme. Tarzan announces himself to the newly arrived white people by leaving a printed message. He warns them, "This Is The House Of Tarzan, The Killer Of Beasts And Many Black Men. Do Not Harm The Things Which Are Tarzan's. Tarzan Watches. Tarzan Of The Apes." (p. 170)

It is Jane, of course, who fully elicits Tarzan's innate emotional and intellectual superiority. Unlike the early movie depictions of a "Me Tarzan, You Jane" relationship, the Tarzan of Burroughs's novel is soon speaking fluently to her, claiming Jane as his love and subsequently discovering his rightful title as Lord Greystroke. Burroughs presents this rapid and remarkable transformation as the inevitable flowering of latent genetic excellence. In describing Tarzan's response to his encounters with the Anglo-Saxon world, he writes, "It was the hallmark of his aristocratic birth, the natural outcropping of many generations of fine breeding, an hereditary instinct of graciousness which a lifetime of uncouth and savage training and environment could not eradicate" (Burroughs, 1912, p. 277).

BURROUGHS ON GENETIC PREDETERMINATION

Burroughs continued to be intrigued with eugenic ideas and proposals. This fascination was expressed in a number of Tarzan sequels. In *Tarzan and the Last Empire* (1929), for example, he creates a city originally overrun with criminals and vagrants. A new emperor, however, establishes a stern policy of genetic laundering. According to Burroughs's story, the emperor

> made laws so drastic that no thief or murderer lived to propagate his kind. Indeed, the laws of Honus Hasta destroyed not only the criminal but all members of his family, so that there were none to transmit to posterity the criminal inclinations of a depraved sire . . . the laws of Honus Hasta prevented the breeding of criminals. (p. 53)

After two millennia of this policy, Tarzan finds a city completely free of crime.

Burroughs's inspiration for the eugenic laws of Honus Hasta appears to have come from a nonfictional source. A month before he began work on *Tarzan and the Last Empire* (1929), Burroughs reported on a 1928 murder trial for the *Los Angeles Examiner.* The defendant, William Hickman, was charged with the brutal murder of a twelve-year-old girl. In his accounts of the trial for the *Examiner,* Burroughs ridiculed the defense argument that Hickman was insane. He wrote that

> Hickman is not normal. But abnormality does not by any means imply insanity. Hickman is a moral imbecile and moral imbecility is not insanity. [The abnormality is genetic—an] inborn brutality of will. . . . If we hang him we have removed . . . a potential menace to peace and happiness and safety of countless future generations, for moral imbeciles breed moral imbeciles, criminals breed criminals, murderers breed murderers just as St. Bernards breed St. Bernards. (cited in Taliaferro, 1999, pp. 229–231)

Burroughs argued that the Hickman case should be a call for a change in social policy regarding "mental defectives." He wrote that

> the city has plenty of moral imbeciles that we might well dispense with . . . a new species of man has been evolving through the ages and only when society awakens . . . will it realize that the members of this new species may not be judged by the same standards that hold for us. . . . Destruction and sterilization are our only defense and we should invoke them while we are yet numerically in the ascendancy. (cited in Taliaferro, 1999, p. 230)

Burroughs was likely encouraged in his claims of moral imbecility by testimony during the trial documenting that there were epileptics, imbeciles, and "constitutional inferiors" in Hickman's family history. Still, his zeal for diagnosing Hickman as mentally inferior and his call for extreme eugenic measures predated and outlasted the case. In an unpublished manuscript he wrote around the time of the trial, Burroughs presents a vision of an idealized civilization of the future. In the article, titled "I See a New Race," he describes the adoption of mandatory intelligence testing and sterilization statutes.

> The sterilization of criminals, defectives and incompetents together with wide dissemination of birth control information and public instruction on eugenics resulted in a rapid rise in the standards of national intelligence after two generations . . . prizes went to the families that produced the most intelligent children. Stupidity became unfashionable. (cited in Porges, 1975, p. 461)

A second unpublished manuscript by Burroughs was found after his death in 1950. Written in 1932, it is yet another novelized account of the crucial struggle in modern society between heredity and environment. It is also Burroughs's testament to the ultimate threat of "bad genes" over "good environment." In the novel, *Pirate Blood*, published posthumously in 1970, John Lafitte and Daisy Juke are college sweethearts. They are also the descendants, respectively, of the infamous pirate Jean Lafitte and "Old Max Juke" of the famous family degeneracy story. Both John and Daisy are fearful of what heredity will mean in their lives. Early in the story they each admit to the "genetic taints" in their family histories. Daisy says, "My people never amount to anything. Dad's the best of the bunch but he's only a poor farmer. He doesn't even believe in education. I wouldn't have gone beyond high school if it hadn't been for mother. I got my looks from her, but I guess the rest of me's Juke." (Burroughs, 1970, p. 72). John complains, "I don't seem to quite make the grade ever. . . . I guess it's the old Mendelian Law at work" (p. 73).

A friend tries to console John Lafitte concerning both his own heredity background and that of Daisy. He criticizes eugenic theory and the fatalistic philosophy it contains. In speaking of Daisy, he says

> It's a horrible theory; it takes all hope from life. What chance would she have with that bloodline back of her—the blood of Old Max Juke that has produced over twelve hundred physical, mental and moral wrecks, paupers, prostitutes, thieves, murderers and other criminals during the past two hundred years? I tell you it was environment that made those people the way they were. (p. 75)

By the end of the story John Lafitte, however, has fallen into a life of crime. He tracks down Daisy, whom he has not seen in years, and discovers that she is a prostitute. "It's the blood, the curse of the blood," Daisy tells John. He tries to comfort her by saying, "We'll get out of this and start over again somewhere." Daisy is inconsolable and says, "I wonder if we can ever escape our putrid blood streams, either here or hereafter" (Burroughs, 1970, p. 172). She leaves the room and a moment later John hears a pistol shot. Daisy has fulfilled her genetic legacy.

BURROUGHS ON BREEDING FOR UTOPIA

In 1933, Burroughs wrote a serialized novel that was originally published in seven installments in *Argosy Weekly*. This story is one of several novels based on trips to Venus by his American hero Carson Napier. In the book, *Lost on Venus* (1963), Napier visits the city of Havatoo, where eugenics is the prevailing law. When he firsts encounters a citizen of Havatoo, Napier is questioned about his homeland. More important, he is questioned about his appearance:

"I've never heard of your country. In fact I have never seen a man before with blue eyes and yellow hair. Are all the people of California like you?"

"Oh, no! There are all colors among us, of hair and eyes and skin. . . ."

"But how can you breed true to type, then?" he demanded.

"We don't," I had to admit.

"Rather shocking," he said to himself. "Immoral—racially immoral." (Burroughs, 1963, p. 274)

In explaining his remarks to Napier, the Venusian describes Havatoo before and after it was taken over by a eugenicist ruler:

Half of our people lived in direst poverty, in vice, in filth; and they breed like flies. The better classes, refusing to bring children into such a world, dwindled rapidly. Ignorance and mediocrity ruled. . . . [The new ruler] wiped out the politicians, and to the positions many of them had filled he appointed the greatest minds of Havatoo—physicists, biologists, chemists, and psychologists.

He encouraged the raising of children by people whom these scientists passed as fit to raise children, and he forbade all others to bear children. He saw to it that the mentally defective were rendered incapable of bringing their like into the world, and no defective infant was allowed to live. (p. 280)

UTOPIA AND DISABILITIES

Utopian visions of human perfection and utopian visions of communities of inclusiveness may be incompatible. The future of disabilities, indeed the future of human diversity, may lie in the resolution of the conflicting visions of human perfection and of a world that values and embraces human variation. The portrayals of human perfection by Disney and by Edgar Rice Burroughs, while different, may be equally dangerous. Whether in *Tarzan, The Hunchback of Notre Dame*, or *Pocahontas*, the Disney version of complex human dramas is sanitized and trivialized. In many ways, it is the corporate entertainment equivalent of telling our children to "look the other way" when encountering profound human differences and their important social implications. On the other hand, Burroughs constantly presents the worldview that a truly utopian society can only be achieved by eliminating the "unfit." Only by freeing society from the clear and present dangers posed by people with diverse and defective characteristics will a new level of human happiness be achieved. While Disney denies differences, Burroughs villainizes them.

The future of disabilities must be explored with an open and clearly focused dialogue concerning the contrasting issues of the scientific amelioration of this form of human diversity and the place of people with disabilities in a humane and inclusive society. The tension between efforts to eliminate the human suffering that has been associated with some forms of disability and efforts that embody a philosophy of genetic quality control is complex and confusing. It deserves, however, our full attention and care. Disability may be a crucible through which the most compelling questions of the future of individuality and the integrity of personhood in general are examined. The answer to the question of whether there is a place or no place for people with disabilities in the future may be a barometer of whether or how diversity and difference in the human experience will survive. In speaking of genetic science in a 1947 essay, C.S. Lewis said of the conquest of nature, "The final stage is come when Man by eugenics . . . has obtained full control over himself. Human nature will be the last part of nature to surrender to Man. . . . The battle will indeed be won. But who precisely will have won it?" (p. 72).

REFERENCES AND FURTHER READINGS

Burroughs, E. R. (1912). *Tarzan of the apes.* New York: A. L. Bust.
Burroughs, E. R. (1929). *Tarzan and the lost empire.* New York: Metropolitan.
Burroughs, E. R. (1930). The Tarzan theme. *Writers Digest*, 10, 29–31.
Burroughs, E. R. (1963). *Lost on Venus.* New York: Dover.
Burroughs, E. R. (1970). *Pirate blood.* Tarzana, CA: Edgar Rice Burroughs, Inc.
Cantillion, R. (1972). *In defense of the fox.* Atlanta, GA: Drake House.
Green, H. (1999, Summer). Xtreme Tarzan. *Disney Magazine*, 32–41.
Kanner, L. (1964). *A history of the care and study of the mentally retarded.* Springfield, IL: Charles C Thomas.
Lewis, C. S. (1947). *The abolition of man.* New York: Macmillan.
Porges, I. (1975). *Edgar Rice Burroughs: The man who created Tarzan.* Provo, UT: Brigham Young University Press.
Smith, J. D. (1987). *The other voices: Profiles of women in the history of special education.* Seattle, WA: Special Child.
Taliaferro, J. (1999). *Tarzan forever: The life of Edgar Rice Burroughs, creator of Tarzan.* New York: Scribner.

13

The Polio Vaccine Research and Children With Disabilities

Sacrifices for the Miracle

The classic fairy tales of Hans Christian Andersen and the Brothers Grimm are testaments to the enduring fascinations and fears that children have shared across the generations. The Grimms' "Hansel and Gretel" and "Cinderella," and Andersen's "The Ugly Duckling" and "The Emperor's New Clothes" continue to entertain children and to reassure them of the ultimate conquest of good over evil. There are other joys and anxieties of childhood, however, which are more generation specific. For the children of the nineties, for example, school violence and the horror of AIDS had an impact unimaginable to previous generations. The decade of the fifties, on the contrary, is often portrayed as a period of idyllic childhood. What is forgotten in the nostalgic accounts of this period, however, is that along with Davy Crockett and coonskin caps, the children of the fifties were taught to crouch under school desks in case of a Russian nuclear attack. Another nightmare for the children of that generation was polio.

Polio, commonly called "infantile paralysis" because it most frequently affected children, reached epidemic proportions in the early fifties. This viral disease paralyzed and killed thousands of children each year. Images of patients and the "iron lungs" used to enable them to breathe terrified both children and their parents. Although the means by which the disease was transmitted was uncertain, swimming pools were closed, public gatherings were avoided, and school cancellations were common during the worst outbreaks.

In early April of 1955, newspaper headlines announced that a safe and effective polio vaccine had been developed by Dr. Jonas Salk. Before the end of that month, thousands of children were vaccinated against polio. By 1961, an oral vaccine for polio had been developed by Dr. Albert Sabin. In 1971, only one case of polio was documented in the United States.

PERSONAL REFLECTIONS ON POLIO

My personal reflections on the terrors of polio are embodied in waves of thoughts and feelings about three occurrences. My first memory is of the death of a boy in my neighborhood. News that Billy had polio came as a shock to the community. He died a few days after the diagnosis. My parents' fears could not be concealed even from a six-year-old. I accepted their restrictions willingly and played alone in my own backyard. I was terrified.

My second recollection is of standing in line for my first polio shot. I watched as some of my friends and classmates were inoculated, dreading my turn. That scene was to be repeated twice before the series of vaccinations was complete. The next time I was vaccinated was as an adult, this time with the Sabin technique. The sugar cube with a dot of vaccine was much more pleasant than the needle.

My final reflection on polio concerns the role of people with disabilities in the development of the polio vaccine. I have only recently become aware of their largely involuntary participation in and exploitation for the research that led to the availability of the vaccine. For my childhood peers and myself, the eradication of polio was a miracle. For people with disabilities, the development of the vaccine is a disturbing saga. For them, it is a story of lives like theirs being judged less valuable than the lives of others, and of lives that were placed at risk involuntarily for the benefit of those others. It is also a testament to the degree to which people with disabilities were viewed as necessary sacrifices to the progress of medicine through most of the last century. Reviewing the story may encourage us to think carefully as we look at the meaning of their lives in the new century.

THE SALK VACCINE AND "INSTITUTIONALIZED" RESEARCH

Vaccination is accomplished by introducing a tiny amount of a virus into the body of the vaccinee. The immune system of the vaccinated person responds by producing antibodies. The vaccinee is thus protected against the "wild" form of the virus and the disease it causes. Vaccines may be created with either a weakened live virus or a dead virus. In general, both weakened and dead viruses produce antibodies but not the disease. Given the unique characteristics of a particular disease, however, either a live or a dead virus vaccine may prove not to be preventative. More important, some vaccines may actually produce the disease that is being targeted for immunity. Research and trials are important, therefore, in producing a safe yet effective vaccine.

Medical research is usually an evolutionary process. The work of one scientist provides a platform or stimulus for the research of the next. One of the pioneers in polio vaccine research was Howard Howe of Johns Hopkins University. In 1952, Howe produced a polio vaccine using a dead virus that he tested on chimpanzees. It seemed to be safe and to produce antibodies against polio. Howe then tested the vaccine on children at the Rosewood Training School in Owings Mills, Maryland. He described these children as "low grade idiots or imbeciles with congenital hydrocephalus, microcephaly, or cerebral palsy" (Howe, 1952, p. 265). In reporting on the response to the vaccine, Howe wrote, "both children under five years of age and chimpanzees develop readily demonstrative neutralizing antibodies . . . following the injection of small quantities of . . . formalin inactivated poliomyelitis virus" (p. 275).

Jonas Salk may have been inspired or nudged by Howe's work to move ahead more quickly with his own work on a vaccine for polio. He might also have been influenced by Howe's research in his selection of subjects for trial vaccinations. Salk had tried his vaccine earlier on animals and it appeared to be safe and effective. In a 1952 article (cited in Chase, 1982), he described testing his vaccine at the D.T. Watson Home for Crippled Children in Pennsylvania. Some of the children he vaccinated had already been disabled by polio and, therefore, had some level of immunity. Others had no immunity at all to the disease. In both groups, Salk found that his vaccine promoted the development of antibodies.

Salk continued his research at the Polk State School in Pennsylvania, where he vaccinated institutionalized children. The antibody production stimulated by the vaccine in this group was also encouraging. He was relieved by the fact that none of the children contracted polio, a risk associated with the vaccine because some undetectable amount of virus might not have been killed. Salk was quoted as saying, "When you inoculate children with polio vaccine, you don't sleep well for two or three months" (Chase, 1982, p. 296).

FEEDING LIVE POLIO VIRUS TO CHILDREN WITH DISABILITIES

The fact that children and adults with disabilities were the subjects of choice for medical research at the time of Salk's work on polio is made even more clear through the trials that led to the development of a live virus vaccine. Although the name of Albert Sabin is most often associated with this vaccine, a number of scientists were involved in its development. In fact, a competition developed between researchers for the discovery of the most reliable and effective oral vaccine. Sabin won the competition, but the race could have been won by Hilary Koprowski.

The quest for a reliable live virus vaccine was stimulated by two factors. One, a live virus vaccine could be administered orally rather than being injected. This would make it less expensive and easier to immunize large numbers of people. Second, Salk's dead virus vaccine had not proven to be as effective as it was originally thought it would be. There were cases where the dead virus did not create immunity. There were also cases where the techniques for killing the virus had not been totally effective. Live virus that remained in the vaccine in these cases had caused polio in some of the people injected with it.

Like Salk and Sabin, Hilary Koprowski had set out on a personal mission to eradicate polio. Even before the successful development of Salk's vaccine, Koprowski was testing weakened, but live, strains of polio virus. He tested the vaccine in monkeys but he also revealed in a 1951 meeting that he had administered a live virus polio vaccine to human subjects.

In his report of feeding the virus to twenty children with mental retardation at Letchworth Village in New York, Koprowski (Koprowski, Norton, & Jervis, 1952) he explained that his decision to administer the virus to humans for the first time was based on "gaps in knowledge concerning the mechanisms of infection and immunity in poliomyelitis . . . due to the fact that, as far as is known, human beings have never been exposed to actual administrations of living poliomyelitis virus for clinical trial purposes" (p 108). Arthur Klein (1972) reported in his description of the trial of the vaccine that Koprowski requested permission of the New York State Department of Health to test it on the children at Letchworth. In fact, Koprowski did not request permission. In his later account of the trials, Koprowski (1997) provided the following recollections:

> I realized then that I would never get official permission from the State of New York. Therefore, we asked permission from the parents of those children. The parents gave us permission to feed vaccine to their children. On February 17, 1950 the first human subject was immunized with poliomyelitis virus by drinking an emulsion. (p. 298)

Koprowski described the vaccinees at Letchworth Village as "volunteers." In fact, "Volunteer No. 1" was a six-year-old boy with severe disabilities who had to be fed the vaccine through a stomach tube. The other nineteen "volunteers" had similar multiple disabilities. There was no mention in the original report of parental permission having been sought or granted.

Fortunately, none of the children at Letchworth developed polio from swallowing the live virus vaccine. Koprowski reported that they all developed antibodies. It is clear, however, that he gambled with the lives of those children. The vaccine strand had been problematic in tests with monkeys. In those earlier trials, in fact, half of the subjects were paralyzed and a quarter had died.

In discussing his memories of the meeting where he had first disclosed his Letchworth Village research, Koprowski (1997) referred to Albert Sabin's reaction:

> Sabin was quite vociferous at the meeting. . . . He questioned my daring. How did I dare to feed children live polio virus. I replied that somebody had to take this step. Well, he turned round and round saying, "How do you dare to use live virus on children? You are not sure about this, you are not sure about that, you may have caused an epidemic. (p. 299)

Koprowski was also criticized in the medical journal *Lancet* in 1952 for the lack of evidence that he had obtained the informed consent of his subjects

> Koprowski et al. tells us in a footnote that for obvious reasons the age, sex, and physical status of each volunteer are not mentioned. The reasons must be more obvious to the authors than to the reader, who can only guess, from the methods used for feeding the virus, that the volunteers were very young and that the volunteering was done by their parents. One of the reasons for the richness of the English language is that the meaning of some words is continually changing. Such a word is "volunteer." We may yet read in a scientific journal that an experiment was carried out with twenty volunteer mice, and that twenty other mice volunteered as controls. ("Poliomyelitis," 1952, p. 552)

This criticism, however, does not seem to have deterred Koprowski. Subsequent investigations of the records from a conference on the "Biology of Poliomyelitis" indicate that several further trials of live virus vaccine were very likely conducted at Letchworth but were not published in the mainstream medical literature.

Koprowski and the Children of Sonoma

It is certain, however, that Koprowski conducted his vaccine research on children with mental retardation elsewhere. In July of 1952, Koprowski tested his oral vaccine on sixty-one children at Sonoma State Hospital in California, all of whom had mental retardation as their primary diagnosis. The children ranged in age from eight months to eight years of age. This time Koprowski made certain that he had formal permission to conduct his research. With the help of physicians at Sonoma, the appropriate clearance was swiftly obtained from California authorities. The trial was considered a success when fifty-two of the sixty-one children showed an increase in antibody levels to polio.

In the course of the vaccine research, Koprowski and his colleagues conducted another study. This experiment is particularly revealing of the attitudes toward children with disabilities that were prevalent during the research. Koprowski reported that a group of six children who had been fed the vaccine were, as a result, excreting virus in their stools. He described them as being kept "in very intimate contact" with another eight children who lacked antibodies. In fact, the children (who were incontinent) were allowed to play together for three hours a day on a plastic mat that, although washed down to remove gross soils, was deliberately not disinfected. In the course of this experiment, three of the unvaccinated children became infected with the virus. None of the nurses, however, developed antibodies. Koprowski reasoned that the nurses caring for the children took precautions against infection, wearing protective clothing and washing their hands after every contact with a child. Koprowski also concluded that the vaccine virus was not contagious "when the principles of simple personal hygiene are practiced" (Koprowski, Norton, & Jervis, 1956, p. 959). Again, the disregard for the children as human beings is evident in this report.

Koprowski continued his research on institutionalized populations, including other children with mental retardation and the infants of female prison inmates, for several years. In 1957 and 1958, he enlarged his research to include thousands of children in Africa and Russia. His vaccine fell into disfavor, however, when polio cases in Northern Ireland were linked to his research there. Ultimately Albert Sabin would win the oral vaccine race, and his form of live virus was adopted for use in the United States.

RESEARCH AND DISABILITIES: OTHER CASES

As disturbing as the history of the polio vaccine trials are, there are other examples of children and adults with disabilities being used as devalued subjects in medical research. During the forties and through the fifties, children and adults at Fernald State School were used in a scientific study conducted by the Massachusetts Institute of Technology on the nutritional effects of ingesting radioactive iron (Allen, 1993a, 1993b). Children who received permission from their parents to join the "Science Club" were fed oatmeal laced with the radiated metal. From 1946 to 1952, over one hundred and twenty-five children were exposed to radiation at the Fernald School in this manner.

The Willowbrook State School was another setting in which the questionable use of persons with disabilities in medical research occurred. The

Willowbrook studies were conducted from the fifties to the seventies, and sought to identify a vaccine for hepatitis. A research team systematically infected residents with varying strands of hepatitis, knowing that those children would develop the infectious disease.

The value placed on people with disabilities by some researchers is evident in their choice of human subjects rather than animals. According to the Humane Society, institutionalized children have been used for research purposes because they are "cheaper than calves." During the polio trials, the cost of raising and keeping monkeys for experimental use was so high that doctors frequently sought human "volunteers." Children were given an experimental vaccine after it had been tested on only sixty-two animals.

In the cases of the Fernald radiation studies and the Willowbrook hepatitis experiment, the validity of the parental consent obtained is questionable. According to the permission letter to the parents in the Fernald experiment, the benefits of the Science Club consisted of receiving an extra quart of milk each day, attendance at baseball games, and trips to the beach. There was no mention in the parental consent letter of radiation experiments nor of the potential harm that could come to their children.

Consent in the Willowbrook studies was also obtained in a questionable manner. Parents were asked for consent and promised that their children would be placed on a special ward with extra staff. The researchers failed to tell the parents that the special ward was for individuals infected with hepatitis.

CLAIMING A PLACE OF VALUE FOR PEOPLE WITH DISABILITIES: THE CONTINUING STRUGGLE

Jonas Salk won a victory over the polio epidemic. Albert Sabin won the race for an oral vaccine. Millions of people in the world benefited from these triumphs. It is critical, however, that we reflect on the struggle that continues for people with disabilities in claiming their human worth in the eyes of their fellow human beings. Perhaps the sacrifice that these people have made for others will eventually be recognized and their value in society secured. Until then, their friends, families, and advocates cannot rest.

REFERENCES AND FURTHER READINGS

Allen, S. (1993a, December 26). Radiation used on retarded: Postwar experiments done at Fernald School. *The Boston Globe,* pp. 1, 45.

Allen, S. (1993b, December 31). MIT records show wider radioactive testing at Fernald. *The Boston Globe,* pp. 1, 13.

Chase, A. (1982). *Magic shots: A human and scientific account of the long and continuing struggle to eradicate infectious diseases by vaccination.* New York: William Morrow.

Grodin, M., & Glantz, L. (1994). *Children as research subjects.* New York: Oxford University Press.

Higgins, R. (1998, January, 18). Haunted by the "Science Club"—monetary offer can't erase his memory. *The Boston Globe,* p. 1.

Hooper, E. (1999). *The river: A journey to the source of HIV and AIDS.* New York: Little, Brown.

Howe, H. (1952). Antibody response of chimpanzees and human beings to formalin inactivated trivalent poliomyelitis vaccine. *American Journal of Hygiene, 55,* 265–279.

Humane Society (n.d.). *Humane vivisection: Foundlings cheaper than animals.* Washington, DC: Author.

Klein, A. (1972). *Trial by fury: The polio vaccine controversy.* New York: Scribner.

Koprowski, H., Jervis, G., & Norton, T. (1952). Immune responses in human volunteers upon oral administration of a rodent adapted strain of poliomyelitis virus. *American Journal of Hygiene, 55,* 108–126.

Koprowski, H., Norton, T., & Jervis, G. (1952). Clinical investigation on attenuated strains of poliomyelitis virus: Use as a method of immunization of children with living virus. *Journal of the American Medical Association, 160,* 954–966.

Koprowski, I. (1997). *A woman wanders through life and science.* Albany: State University of New York Press.

Paul, J. (1971). *A history of poliomyelitis.* New Haven, CT: Yale University Press.

Poliomyelitis: A new approach. (1952). *Lancet, 1*(i), 552.

Rogers, N. (1992). *Dirt and disease: Polio since FDR.* New Brunswick, NJ: Rutgers University Press.

Part II
Questions to Ponder

1. Was the eugenics movement in the United States led by evil men and women? If not, what were they trying to accomplish? Did they believe they were doing the "right thing"? Why?

2. What are the most important lessons the eugenics movement offers us today?

3. Are there parallels between the issues raised by the eugenics movement and those being raised today by the Human Genome Project, especially in relation to the genetic engineering capabilities that are now being developed?

4. Are people with disabilities contributing members of society? In what ways?

5. Do you believe that eugenic attitudes are widely held in the United States today? What evidence or examples can you find to support your belief?

Part III

Disability in Historical and Literary Perspectives

During my childhood and adolescence, I was often reminded by my parents that I should "count my blessings." The reminder was intended to help keep me from taking for granted my good fortune, and to discourage me from self-pity over minor disappointments. As an adult, however, I do not practice counting blessings. On the contrary, I have come to believe that blessings are not things, quantifiable possessions, that can be measured, classified, or tallied.

Each blessing is incomparable. There are no "small blessings." All blessings are of immeasurable value. One of the blessings that I increasingly cherish is the joy of discovery. Another is the pleasure of sharing discoveries.

The stories in this part of *In Search of Better Angels* are accounts of discoveries that came to me as blessings. Each is a story I discovered while searching for something else. The serendipity of coming across an unexpected and intriguing reference while doing research on an unrelated topic is a thrilling experience. Stumbling upon a book on a library shelf that leads to new revelations can be a gratifying accident.

During my work as a teacher and scholar, I have been encouraged to go on adventures of discovery by friends, teachers, and family. I hope that the stories in this part of my book will be of interest to you, the reader. I trust that you will share in the excitement of gaining insights into the minds and hearts of the scientists, writers, and people with disabilities the stories portray. In addition, I hope that these stories will encourage your interest in examining the meaning of human disability through literary and historical perspectives.

14

Disability and the Need for a Romantic Science

Darwin's Last Child

The term *eugenics*, derived from the Greek word *eugenes*, meaning well-born, was first used by Francis Galton in 1883 to describe what he envisioned as a new discipline. He defined *eugenics* as a science through which the influences that could improve the inborn qualities of races and classes of human beings could be discovered. One of the primary aims of eugenicists was the elimination from human populations of unwanted hereditary disorders through the use of selective marriage practices. Quickly, however, the movement also embraced the promotion of compulsory sterilization of people with traits that were judged to be undesirable, institutionalization of people diagnosed as defective, and restrictions on the immigration of people whose race or nationality was deemed to possess inferior hereditary qualities.

Galton was a cousin of Charles Darwin. It is not surprising, therefore, that the concepts and language of the theory of evolution were associated with eugenics from its inception. The discourse on social policy regarding mental retardation and other disabilities in the late nineteenth and early twentieth centuries was filled with references to the survival of the fittest and the struggle for existence. Eugenics was applied science founded on the central biological theory of the time—evolution. Eugenicists were obsessed with the elimination of people who were considered defective, and they viewed public policy that promoted the welfare of people with disabilities as an interference with the process of natural selection.

Darwin made references to mental retardation in his major work on human evolution, *The Descent of Man* (1871). He compared what he observed to be the imitative behavior of people with mental retardation to the behavior of our "nearest allies, the monkeys" and the "barbarous races of mankind" (p. 133). Darwin drew other parallels between the behavior of people with mental retardation and animals. He described them as smelling their food like animals before eating it and cited a reference to an "idiot . . . smelling every mouthful of food before eating it" (p. 53). Darwin closed his discussion by describing people with mental retardation as having filthy habits, having no sense of decency, and, like animals, having remarkably hairy bodies.

Darwin conceived of people with mental retardation as evolutionary mistakes. He speculated that retardation resulted from reversions in the developmental process. From his perspective, persons with mental retardation displayed the characteristics of other species and what he considered to be inferior races of human beings. They had reverted to these life forms even though they were born to parents of a superior level of evolutionary development. For reasons that were not clear to him, something had caused an error in reproduction that resulted in an individual who looked and behaved like a member of an inferior species.

A similar concept was developed by J. Langdon Down in his theory of the racial nature of mental retardation. Darwin's influence is very evident in Down's observations on what was to become known as Down syndrome and that he termed "mongolian idiocy." In his 1866 essay, "Observations on an Ethnic Classification of Idiots," Down described children and adults that he thought were the products of "degeneracy." Although he provided little detail on the mechanisms of this phenomenon, Down theorized that in the case of "mongolism" the evolutionary degeneracy was caused most often by "tuberculosis in the parents."

Charles Darwin became an icon for scientific explanations of both biological and social phenomena. Thus, his impact on scientific and public perceptions of disability has been enormous. The theory of evolution, as interpreted through social Darwinism, had tremendous consequences for hundreds of thousands of people. Arguments concerning the meaning of disability, and the political and economic responses to that meaning, are still influenced by Darwin's observations and their derivatives. There is, however, another facet to what we know about Darwin's understanding of the human issues associated with disability. Through his relationship with his youngest child, a boy with mental retardation, we are able to see a different and contradictory view. Through the prism of personal experience, this giant of the scientific world viewed mental retardation in a different light.

Lewis Thomas, in his 1979 book *The Medusa and the Snail*, expressed misgivings about a total reliance on science for knowledge. He explained, "The only solid piece of scientific truth about which I am totally confident is that we are profoundly ignorant about nature" (p. 73). Michael Merleau-Ponty (1963) also commented on expanding our vision of knowledge:

> I cannot shut myself up within the realm of science. All my knowl-
> edge of the world, even scientific knowledge, is gained from my
> own particular point of view, or from some experience of the
> world. . . . The whole universe of science is built upon the world as
> directly experienced. . . . We must begin by reawakening the basic
> experience of the world. (p. viii)

At the time that Darwin was working on *The Origin of Species*, the book that would establish his place in the history of science, he was also worried about the health of his children. He had been preoccupied with his own health throughout his life and feared that his marriage to his cousin, Emma Edgewood, placed their children at special risk for "hereditary ill-health." Indeed, several of their children did suffer with chronic illnesses. Darwin was deeply and continually concerned for his ailing children and for the illnesses that Emma experienced. One of the most agonizing aspects of his family life, however, came with the birth of his last child, Charles Waring Darwin, who was his namesake.

Emma conceived this child when she was 48 years old. She was apparently quite uncomfortable and uneasy during the pregnancy. A description of her discomfort, and a comment about the new baby and his fate, was recorded by Darwin's daughter Henrietta (Darwin, 1858).

> This had been a suffering year for my mother. Her last child,
> Charles Waring Darwin, was born on December 6th, 1856. I
> remember very well the weary months she passed, and reading
> aloud to her sometimes to help her bear her discomforts. The poor
> little baby was born without its full share of intelligence. Both my
> mother and father were infinitely tender towards him but, when he
> died in the summer of 1858, after their first sorrow, they could only
> feel thankful. He had never learnt [sic] to walk or talk. (p. 521)

The baby's disability was apparently noticed quickly by the Darwins. Although there is no documentation that sufficiently describes the nature of the child's mental retardation, it has been speculated, largely on the basis of Emma's age, that Charles Waring had Down syndrome. Regardless of diagnosis and cause, however, Darwin wrote a sensitive and detailed description of his son as a memorial to him following his death.

His words reveal his deep love of the child and elucidate the impressions of his daughter Henrietta.

> Our poor baby was born December 6th, 1856 and died on June 28th, 1858, and was therefore above 18 months old. He was small for his age and backward in walking and talking, but intelligent and observant. When crawling naked on the floor he looked very elegant. He had never been ill and cried less than any of our babies. He was of a remarkably sweet, placid and joyful disposition; but had not high spirits, and did not laugh much. He often made strange grimaces and shivered, when excited; but did so also, for a joke and his little eyes used to glisten, after pouting out or stretching widely his little lips. He used sometimes to move his mouth as if talking loudly, but making no noise, and this he did when very happy. He was particularly fond of standing on one of my hands and being tossed in the air; and then he always smiled, and made a little pleased noise. I had just taught him to kiss me with open mouth, when I told him. He would lie for a long time placidly on my lap looking with a steady and pleased expression at my face; sometimes trying to poke his poor little fingers into my mouth, or making nice little bubbling noises as I moved his chin. I had taught him not to scratch, but when I said, "Giddlums never scratches now" he could not always resist a little grab, and then he would look at me with a wicked little smile. He would play for any length of time on the sofa, letting himself fall suddenly, and looking over his shoulder to see that I was ready. He was very affectionate and had a passion for Parslow [the Darwin's butler] and it was very pretty to see his extreme eagerness with outstretched arms, to get to him. Our poor little darling's short life has been placid, innocent and joyful. I think and trust he did not suffer so much at last, as he appeared to do; but the last 36 hours were miserable beyond expression. In the sleep of Death he resumed his placid looks. (p. 521)

These beautiful and caring words of a father for his lost child are a testament to the value of a child with a disability to his family. They are the most poignant and moving expressions that I have read from this genius of modern science. They remind me of the contributions that people with disabilities often make to their parents, siblings, and communities. The words stand in stark contrast to Darwin's description of the similarities of persons with mental retardation to animals. They provide an important glimpse of the human side of our knowledge of what disabilities are and how they should be constructed for others to understand. His words remind us that social definitions and roles are created by the personal meaning we have for one another.

Simi Linton (1998) issued a call for conceptualizing disabilities in a way that more completely recognizes the natural spectrum of human diversity.

To achieve a full appreciation of the complimentarity and interdependence of people, the eyes of both science and passion are required. Commenting on the work of Nobel laureate and geneticist, Barbara McClintock, Linton wrote, "If something doesn't fit there's a reason, and you find what it is. Rather than overlook difference, for instance, by naming an exception an aberration, a contaminant, she worked to understand its place and function" (p. 120). It appears that Darwin's last son taught him in a personal sense that mental retardation was not an aberration or a contaminant.

In his 1983 book *Awakenings*, Oliver Sacks wrote that he once asked A. R. Luria what he considered to be the most interesting thing in the world. Luria replied, "I cannot express it in one word, I have to use two. I would have to speak of 'romantic science.' It has been my life's hope to found or refound a romantic science" (p. 523). In recent years, some critics of the effort to redefine and reconceptualize disabilities have called for a dichotomous separation between a scientific understanding of disabilities and the romance of disability advocacy and activism. On the contrary, it seems to me, it is crucial to the lives of millions of people that we create a "romantic science" of disability.

REFERENCES AND FURTHER READINGS

Bowlby, J. (1990). *Charles Darwin: A new life.* New York: W. W. Norton.

Colp, R. (1977). *To be an invalid: The illness of Charles Darwin.* Chicago: University of Chicago Press.

Darwin, C. (1858). The death of Charles Waring Darwin. In F. Burkhardt & S. Smith (Eds.), *The correspondence of Charles Darwin* (Vol. 7). New York: Cambridge University Press.

Darwin, C. (1871). *The descent of man.* London: Murray.

Davis, L. (1995). *Enforcing normalcy: Disability, deafness and the body.* New York: Verso.

Down, J. L. H. (1866). Observations on an ethnic classification of idiots. Reprinted In T. E. Jordan (1966), *Perspectives in mental retardation* (pp. 259–262). Carbondale: Southern Illinois University Press.

Linton, S. (1998). *Claiming disability: Knowledge and identity.* New York: New York University Press.

Litchfield, H. (Ed.). (1915). *Emma Darwin: A century of family letters.* New York: Littleton.

Merleau-Ponty, M. (1963). *Phenomenology of perception.* London: Routledge & Kegan Paul.

Sacks, O. (1983). *Awakenings.* New York: Dutton.

Smith, J. D. (1985). *Minds made feeble: The myth and legacy of the Kallikaks.* Rockville, MD: Aspen.

Thomas, L. (1979). *The medusa and the snail.* New York: Viking.

White, M., & Gribben, J. (1996). *Darwin: A life in science.* New York: Dutton.

15

Words of Understanding, Concepts of Inclusiveness

The Wisdom of Margaret Mead

Margaret Mead is recognized as one of the founders of American anthropology. Her fame is usually associated, of course, with her work in the South Pacific. Mead's study of adolescence in Polynesian cultures resulted in the 1928 publication of her classic book, *Coming of Age in Samoa.* In that book, she questioned the widely accepted view that adolescence is a biologically induced period of inevitable developmental trauma and struggle. In contrast, Mead presented a picture of adolescence in Samoa that was largely carefree and happy. She also argued that many other of the developmental characteristics that were being described in Western cultures at that time as biologically determined were, in fact, products of culture. From this perspective, Mead asserted, these traits were subject to change based on cultural choice.

Margaret Mead's work was highly controversial from the beginning and aroused the ire of many of the scientists who were convinced of the hereditary determination of psychological and sociological traits in human beings. Her work has continued to be scrutinized and criticized, along with claims that her writings were more ideological than scientific. She has also been criticized as an anthropologist for her involvement in psychological rather than anthropological issues. It is interesting to note, therefore, that Mead's original graduate training was in psychology, not anthropology. It is also important to understand that there were aspects of her early work that engaged questions that are still debated. In addition, some of Margaret Mead's insights on disabilities later in her career merit highlighting.

In 1923, Mead conducted thesis research for her first graduate degree, a master's in psychology from Columbia University. She chose a topic that was related to the biological determinism that dominated American psychology at the time, the heredity of intelligence. Eminent psychologists such as Henry Goddard and Lewis Terman asserted that intelligence was largely a genetic trait that could be validly measured, even in minority groups, through the use of intelligence tests. Margaret Mead, within the context of this prevailing scientific assumption, selected for her thesis a study of intelligence test scores of children of Italian immigrant families.

Mead's choice of Italian immigrants for her study is quite understandable given her background. As a child she had lived for a number of years in Hammonton, New Jersey, a community near Philadelphia with a large Italian population. Her family moved there to accommodate the research of Margaret's mother, Emily Fogg Mead, a sociologist. Emily was doing research for her doctoral degree at the University of Pennsylvania. Her study was focused on a comparison of the adaptations of Italian immigrants to their lives in rural and urban communities in America.

In the first two decades of the twentieth century, intelligence testing had become very important in American psychology. It was particularly central to the widely held belief in the hereditary etiology of mild mental retardation. Intelligence tests were used to justify the institutionalization and sterilization of people who were seen as eugenic threats to the integrity of the culture. Intelligence tests were also given to immigrants being processed for entry into the United States through Ellis Island. The results were claimed as evidence that most Jewish, Hungarian, and Italian immigrants coming to the United States were feebleminded.

In her autobiographical book *Blackberry Winter,* Mead (1972) spoke of her thesis. During that period, she wrote,

> I was not only preparing to take a PhD in anthropology but also completing my Master's essay in psychology. There were many tiresome statistics to do, as I correlated the scores on intelligence tests made by Hammonton Italian children with the amount of Italian spoken in their homes. (p. 122)

In analyzing the results of her research, Mead found that the intelligence test performance of the Italian children was clearly inferior to the test performance of American children. This finding was consistent with the reports of psychologists who, on the basis of similar test results, had earlier claimed that immigrants were intellectually inferior. The focus of Mead's study, however, went beyond the differences in test performance. Through examining other variables, she uncovered important differences within her subject group of two hundred and seventy-six Italian children. She found that there were strong correlations among intelligence scores, the language spoken at home, the date of immigration of the father, and the social status of the families.

Through her study of the test results and the family biographies of the students, Margaret Mead came to understand what seems in one sense so obvious but in another sense so elusive regarding the influence of cultural and family environments on development. She noted that

1. The Italians are definitely inferior in performance to the Americans if judged by the test showing alone. Therefore, if grading or promotion were to be governed by test results the Italians would be placed at a clear disadvantage

2. The scores of the Italian children have been shown to be influenced by the language factor . . . according to the language spoken at home, the social status and the length of time the father has been in this country, this last factor being somewhat interwoven with the language factor. . . . Classification of foreign children in schools where they have to compete with American children, on the basis of group intelligence findings alone, is not a just evaluation of the child's innate capacity. (Mead, 1927, p. 468)

Viewed from the vantage point of more than seventy years following her observations, Mead's analysis seems wise and prudent. It is sobering to recognize, however, that seven decades later the basis of her call for justice is still being debated. Intelligence test results are still being hailed in some scientific and political circles as hallmarks of deficiency in some racial and ethnic groups.

The fact that Margaret Mead did not consider the Italian children she tested to be defective is perhaps best reflected in the opening sentences of one of the appendices to *Coming of Age in Samoa* (1928). Here she referred to herself as a person without any training in diagnosis—and without any apparatus for exact diagnosis of the mentally defective. Her humility and her recognition of the multicultural complexities of mental retardation in this passage are, however, eclipsed by the thought-provoking information she reported on the prevalence of mental retardation in the island society she was studying.

In the Manua Archipelago with a population of a little over two thousand people, I saw one case which would be classified as idiocy, one imbecile, one boy of fourteen who appeared to be both feeble-minded and insane. . . . The idiot child was one of seven children; he had a younger brother who had walked for over a year, and the mother declared that there were two years between the children. . . . In no one of these three cases of definite mental deficiency was there any family history which threw any light upon the matter. (p. 155)

In her Samoa study, Mead reported two additional cases of disabilities. One was of a boy with epilepsy who died while she was there. The other was a girl of ten who was paralyzed below her waist and may have had other disabilities resulting from poisoning. It is intriguing to consider the cultural differences in the prevalence of disabilities implied by Mead's report from Samoa.

For example, the total of five people that she described in terms of a classification of mental retardation out of a population of two thousand yields a prevalence figure of less than .002%. This is, of course, far below the most conservative figures for mental retardation that have been reported in recent years in the United States.

The observations of an anthropologist with training in psychology and psychometrics yielded a mental retardation prevalence figure that is minuscule and puzzling when compared to our contemporary under-standing of the needs and characteristics that constitute what we call mental retardation. Where were the other people in Mead's study of Samoa who would be similar to those people we think of today in our country as having mental retardation? A clue may lie in Mead's discussion of Sala. In the appendix to her book, she described this girl as standing out from the other adolescent girls she observed in Samoa. Mead referred her readers back to her earlier characterization of Sala as "sufficiently inferior to the general norm of intelligence to approximate to a moron" (p. 155).

In *Coming of Age in Samoa* (1928), Mead described Sala in the chapter titled "The Girl in Conflict." According to Mead, Sala was:

stupid, underhanded, deceitful and she possessed no aptitude for the simplest mechanical tasks. Her ineptness was the laughing stock of the village and her lovers were many and casual, the fathers of illegitimate children, men whose wives were temporarily absent, witless boys bent on a frolic. It was a saying among the girls of the village that Sala was apt at only one art, sex, and that she, who couldn't even sew thatch or weave blinds, would never get a husband. (p. 181)

These frank descriptions belie the insight and compassion for Sala that Margaret Mead revealed later in her description of the young woman's plight. Even while portraying her as fickle and superficial in relationships, Mead suggested that there was more depth to Sala's comprehension of her own incompetence than her peers may have understood. Of Sala's understanding of her place in the Samoan village that was her home, Mead noted that

> The social attitude towards her was one of contempt, rather than antagonism, and she had experienced it keenly enough to have sunk very low in her own eyes. She had a sullen furtive manner, lied extravagantly in her assertions of skill and knowledge, and was ever on the alert for slights and possible innuendoes. (p. 181)

In describing Sala and her station in her Samoan village, however, Mead also provided a suggestion that the young girl's life in that setting was quite different from the perceived place of the moron in America that had been prescribed a few years earlier by the psychologist Henry Goddard. Goddard (1912) had said that there was no place in the complex structure of twentieth-century America for morons. In his description of the need for institutionalization of the Salas in the United States, Goddard stated that segregation through colonization seemed, given the present state of our knowledge, to be the ideal and perfectly satisfactory method for dealing with these people. In contrast, Mead described a Samoan culture that showed more charity toward weakness than toward misdirected strength. She indicated that even with the negative responses Sala's behavior elicited from others, her well-being in the Samoan culture was ultimately based on a social compact of inclusiveness.

Mead returned to this theme many years later. In 1959, she spoke to a conference sponsored by the American Association on Mental Deficiency (AAMD) (Mead, 1959). In her remarks, she referred to a statement made by a group of Catholic sisters who worked with children who had mental retardation. Mead quoted them as saying that they were attempting to make it possible for the children that they cared for to make a contribution in time as well as in eternity.

Later in her speech, Mead returned to the example of the work of the Catholic Church with people with disabilities. She gave the example of a child with Down syndrome who had been tested, diagnosed, and given every opportunity for the best skill training that money could buy. In her early teens, however, when this young woman was given religious instruction, Mead described the change that took place in the girl's life. She said that at this time the girl

> became Catholic, she became a human being in a way that she had not been one before. . . . I think that what happened on the secular side with this little girl was that for the first time she met a situation where people were willing to teach her the *whole* instead of saying, "you are defective and you can only learn a part." (p. 260)

Mead concluded her address to the AAMD by elaborating on the concept of education for wholeness. She distinguished between societies where everyone participates in all aspects of the culture (e.g., Samoa) and those segmented, socially stratified societies that no longer attempt to teach the whole to all people (e.g., the United States). She emphasized that genuine opportunities are necessary for a culture in which most individuals learn to fully participate, and she warned of the risks of complicating sections of our culture so much that we define them as things most people can't learn.

The greatest challenge advocates for people with disabilities face today are revealed in Margaret Mead's insights. In order to enable people with disabilities to become genuinely included in our culture, we must strive to make accessible to all of them the essential wholeness of citizenship. One step toward promoting this wholeness lies in striving to achieve the Samoan source of hope for Sala, the expression of charity toward weakness.

REFERENCES AND FURTHER READINGS

Freeman, D. (1983). *Margaret Mead and Samoa: The making and unmaking of an anthropological myth.* Cambridge, MA: Harvard University Press.

Goddard, H. (1912). *The Kallikak family: A study in the heredity of feeble-mindedness.* New York: Macmillan.

Herrnstein, R., & Murray, C. (1994). *The bell curve: Intelligence and class structure in American life.* New York: The Free Press.

Juliani, R. N. (1988). Neglected continuities in social research: Emily Fogg Mead, Margaret Mead, and the Italians of Hammonton, New Jersey. *New Jersey Folk Life, 13,* 3–9.

Mead, M. (1927). Group intelligence tests and linguistic disability among Italian children. *School and Society, 25,* 465–468.

Mead, M. (1928). *Coming of age in Samoa: A psychological study of primitive youth for Western civilization.* New York: William Morrow.

Mead, M. (1959). Research cult: Or cure? *American Journal of Mental Deficiency, 64,* 253–264.

Mead, M. (1972). *Blackberry winter: My earlier years.* New York: William Morrow.

Smith, J. D. (1985). *Minds made feeble: The myth and the legacy of the Kallikaks.* Rockville, MD: Aspen.

Smith, J. D., & Nelson, K. (1989). *The sterilization of Carrie Buck.* Far Hill, NJ: New Horizon.

Torrey, F. (1992). *Freudian fraud: The malignant effect of Freud's theory on American thought and culture.* New York: HarperCollins.

16

The Question of Differential Advocacy

Laura Bridgman

CONSTRUCTING THE
DISABILITY OF MENTAL RETARDATION

In his 1994 book, *Inventing the Feeble Mind,* James Trent examines the changing American construction of the meaning of *mental retardation*. He begins his examination with Simple Simon, the nursery rhyme. The rhyme first became popular in the United States during the post-revolutionary period, and Simple Simon illustrates, Trent says, that simpletons were ridiculed and teased but not feared. Trent reports, in fact, that simpletons were a known and expected part of the farm and village life of early American culture.

As life in the United States became more urban and industrial, the simpleton was transformed into the idiot, the imbecile, and, eventually, the moron. These forms and levels of what was known as feeblemindedness implied pathology and required containment. That containment was provided through the social and political creation of residential institutions for people with mental retardation. Institutions came to dominate the public understanding of retardation for many decades.

Trent argues that mental retardation was constructed within the context of the residential institution, for different reasons and with varying meanings. It was defined sometimes in the name of science and at other times in the name of care. In some instances, mental retardation was defined in the name of social control. He finds that the goals of care and control were often commingled in the missions of these institutions. What was provided as care for people who could not adequately manage for themselves was also rationalized as being of service to society. It provided economic and social protection. Trent observes, however, that what was done in the name of care and protection actually diminished resources, status, and power in the lives of institutionalized people. The economic vulnerability of these people shaped their treatment in American society.

In *Abandoned to Their Fate* (1994), Philip Ferguson speaks of mental retardation from another perspective. He describes the impact of the judgment of chronicity on the lives of people considered to be retarded. Through his study of mental retardation in the nineteenth and early twentieth centuries, Ferguson found that to be judged "chronic" meant to be socially abandoned. In Ferguson's words, the judgment of chronicity is reached when "badness becomes incorrigible, ugliness becomes inhuman, and uselessness becomes untrainable" (p. 16). Accordingly, it is the status of chronicity, not that of disability, that has determined the fate of generations of people.

DISABILITY AND INVISIBILITY

When the writer Ralph Ellison died in 1994, a great deal of media attention was focused on his novel, *Invisible Man*. That book, first published in 1952, is not, as the title suggests, science fiction. It is an autobiography of a young man of African American heritage. Through it, he relates his experiences of social and personal isolation. In the opening sentence, Ellison's character declares,

> I am an invisible man. No, I am not a spook like those who haunted Edgar Allan Poe; nor am I one of your Hollywood-movie ectoplasms. I am a man of substance, of flesh and bone, fiber and liquids—and I might even be said to possess a mind. I am invisible, understand, simply because people refuse to see me. (p. 2)

Ellison's character goes on to explain that his invisibility is created because others view him with eyes that are dominated by prejudice, bias, and false assumptions.

> That invisibility to which I refer occurs because of a peculiar disposition of the eyes of those with whom I come in contact. A matter of the construction of their inner eyes . . . you often doubt if you really exist. You wonder whether you aren't simply a phantom in other people's minds. (p. 3)

Ellison's powerful words about the construction of "inner eyes" helped his readers understand in a new way the experience of race as more than a set of physical characteristics or a shared social history.

Ellison demonstrated that the meaning of ethnic differences has often been constructed by powerful majority groups in ways that have resulted in oppression and racism. There has also been a long history of the social construction of the meaning of *disability*. These constructions have contributed to the invisibility of persons with disabilities in ways that are analogous to the invisibility created by racism. It is interesting to note, however, that the degree of this invisibility may be determined by the type of disability. It is also important to understand that people with different disabilities have not always been united by their shared experiences. Instead, it is evident that invisibility has sometimes existed just as strikingly between people with different disabilities as between people with and without disabilities.

People with mental retardation have been among the most socially invisible of all people with disabilities. A revealing example of this difference in the valuing of, and advocacy for, people with mental retardation is to be found in accounts of the life of Laura Bridgman.

LAURA BRIDGMAN: THE FIRST MIRACLE

Laura Bridgman was born into a prominent Massachusetts family in 1829. At the age of two, scarlet fever rendered her deaf and blind, as well as unable to smell or taste very well. She was, therefore, virtually unable to communicate with the world around her except through her sense of touch. In 1837, she came to live at Perkins Institute for the Blind in Boston. There, she was tutored by the founder of the school, Samuel Gridley Howe. Howe devised a teaching method that built on Laura Bridgman's ability to feel the differences in the shapes of objects. Through drill and practice in distinguishing shapes that were familiar to her, he led her to the understanding that these objects could be given names. At first he used labels with raised print on them to assign the names that Laura came to comprehend. He then taught her to form these words using movable letters. He was thus teaching her by methods similar to those that were used for other students at Perkins who were blind. Eventually, however, he shifted to a communication method that had been developed for students who were deaf. He began teaching her words using fingerspelling. He spelled words into her hand and then associated them with objects and actions. This was the method, of course, that would later come to be associated with Anne Sullivan's teaching of Helen Keller.

Laura's fame and Howe's successful teaching were later eclipsed, in fact, by the extraordinary accomplishments of Anne Sullivan and Helen Keller. It is ironic that little note has been taken of the fact that Anne Sullivan, herself a student at Perkins, learned to communicate with Laura

Bridgman, and then applied what she had learned in her teaching of Helen Keller.

For several decades during the nineteenth century, however, Laura Bridgman attracted international attention, and Samuel Gridley Howe's work with her was heralded with as much admiration as the Miracle Worker, Anne Sullivan, would later receive. To many American intellectuals she became a symbol, exemplifying the power of enlightened educational techniques and their capacity to transform seemingly hopeless cases. She was held up as a model of Victorian womanhood because of her courage and intelligence in the face of grave challenges. Some girls reportedly admired her so much that they poked their dolls' eyes out and named them Laura. Reluctant young students were reminded to always compare their own efforts with those of the little deaf and blind girl who had accomplished so much in the face of such overwhelming obstacles.

Howe's accounts of Laura Bridgman's education, published in the yearly reports of the Perkins Institution, attracted the attention of leading philosophers, theologians, and writers of the time. Historians who have studied Howe's reports are convinced that he recognized from the beginning of his work with Laura Bridgman that her education would be of interest in scholarly circles. His efforts to teach her may have been motivated by the deepest altruism, but, according to Edwin Freeburg (1992), "Howe recognized from the start that Laura Bridgman was not just another afflicted child in need, but an object of peculiar interest" (p. 194). He surely realized that if he were to succeed in teaching her to communicate, his work would have far-reaching religious and philosophical implications that would capture the attention of the world.

Laura Bridgman and the Tabula Rasa Theory

For more than a century, John Locke's argument concerning the mind as a blank slate had dominated philosophy. The mind, according to Locke, was created by the experiential "writings" on that slate. The senses, therefore, determined the material character of the mind. If this portrait of the mind was accurate, then Howe would find that Laura Bridgman's mind was empty of all images, including moral and religious formulations. On the contrary, as Howe began to communicate with her about ideas, he found that her mind was not a tabula rasa. He described her internal life as a soul jailed in a body that was "active, and struggling continually not only to put itself in communication with things without, but to manifest what is going on within itself" (Howe, 1893, p. 9). Howe described Laura's internal life, as he discovered it in its natural and untouched state, as being of the highest moral character. He found that "her moral sense, is remarkably acute; few children are so affectionate or so scrupulously conscientious, few are so sensible of their own rights or regardful of the rights of others" (Howe, 1893, p. 50).

Laura Bridgman and the Question
of "Differential Advocacy"

To support his argument that Laura Bridgman was innately moral, he described her behavior toward other people after she had been liberated by his teaching and thus enabled to communicate. He reported that she was always eager to share with others and to help take care of sick people. He also said that she showed a keen sense of sympathy for people with disabilities. Howe noted, however, one exception to her natural expressions of natural altruism. He said that she showed an "unamiable" lack of respect for the children at the Perkins Institution whom she considered to be mentally inferior to herself. Interpreting this as an understandable manifestation of her Anglo-Saxon heritage, he excused the advantage she took of these children when she expected them to "wait on her" (p. 20).

One of the most famous of Laura Bridgman's powerful and influential visitors at Perkins was Charles Dickens. His admiration for her began when he read Howe's accounts of instructing her. It increased when Dickens visited her in Boston. For Charles Dickens, Laura Bridgman was "both charming and inspirational: a merry, graceful, and intelligent young girl, she seemed also to symbolize the possibility of spiritual awakening and redemption" (1842, p. 163). Dickens described his visit to Laura at Perkins in *American Notes* (1842). He related his impressions of her, and he also quoted from Howe's reports. In his account, Dickens (1842) repeats Howe's observation that she had disdain for those children that she believed to be intellectually inferior.

> It has been remarked in former reports that she can distinguish different degrees of intellect in others, and that she soon regarded almost with contempt, a new-comer, when, after a few days, she discovered her weakness of mind. This unamiable part of her character has been more strongly developed during the past year. She chooses for her friends and companions, those children who are intelligent, and can talk best with her; and she evidently dislikes to be with those who are deficient in intellect, unless, indeed, she can make them serve her purposes, which she is evidently inclined to do. (p. 39)

Laura Bridgman was not the only student with both deafness and blindness that Samuel Howe attempted to teach. He was moderately successful in teaching a twelve-year-old boy, Oliver Caswell, who had these disabilities He worked with the two of them together at times and found Oliver "more affectionate and sympathetic than Laura, but not as quick or curious" (Meltzer, 1964, p. 101). Two other pupils with deaf-blindness spent short periods at Perkins with less satisfactory results. One, Lucy Reed, was judged to have "subnormal intelligence."

Samuel Gridley Howe is a person of importance in the history of disabilities. In addition to his work with students with blindness and deaf-blindness, he was an early advocate for the education of students with mental retardation. He convinced the legislature of Massachusetts to provide funding for a school for the "teaching and training of idiotic children" in October of 1848 (M. Howe & Hall, 1904, p. 229). The school was initially housed at Perkins Institute. According to two of his daughters, however, Howe soon discovered that his blind students resented deeply the presence of the students with mental retardation under their roof (M. Howe & Hall, 1904, p. 229). His daughters interpreted this resentment as an expression of fear that they might come to be associated with the retardation of these "weaker brethren." They quote Laura Bridgman's journal as evidence of this feeling of resentment. Laura Bridgman expressed the hope that the students with mental retardation would not actually come to Perkins and the fear that if they did they would "have our rooms . . . [and] our nice sitting room in a few days" (p. 231).

Stigma by Association

Laura Bridgman's fears regarding the perceived association between herself and her "weaker brethren" may not have been unfounded. Indeed, a literature has developed around the very notion of the transferability of social stigma; the process in which a "normal" person is seen by others as possessing the characteristics of a stigma merely by a close association with a stigmatized other. Erving Goffman (1963) has written about the acquisition of a social stigma by affiliation. Research has accumulated on the varying contexts in which stigma by association operates. These findings indicate that students portrayed as having fathers that were depressed, alcoholic, or incarcerated were perceived to have more serious living-adjustment problems in college than those portrayed as having non-stigmatized fathers. In two experiments conducted by Stephen Neuberg (Neuberg, Smith, Hoffman, & Russell, 1994), the process of stigma by association was further elucidated. People clearly identified as heterosexual were perceived as less sociable (e.g., friendly, likable) and less civil (e.g., trustworthy or honest) when viewed conversing with persons identified as being homosexual. Was Laura Bridgman's resentment toward having to share close quarters with mentally retarded people an effort to avoid the acquisition of yet another stigma?

There is evidence to suggest that mental retardation carries the most debilitating socially constructed disability stigma; more so than alcoholism, depression, crime, or sexual orientation. As Robert Edgerton (1967) points out: "One might speculate that no other stigma is as basic as mental retardation in the sense that a person so labeled is thought to be so completely lacking in basic competence" (p. 184). Other research indicates that people with mental retardation are themselves acutely aware of this stigma and tend to react with derogation of their peers' social competence and physical attractiveness.

It may also be the threat of being socially ostracized that leads some families to engage in behaviors that minimize the threat of associated stigma. Arnold Birenbaum (1970) has commented extensively on the great lengths that parents of children with mental retardation may go to in an attempt to maintain the appearance of a nonstigmatized or "normal" family lifestyle. He concludes that some parents avoid agencies that provide needed services in order to maintain the appearance they have of a "conventional" family lifestyle.

Laura Bridgman may have been acutely aware of the very real potential of being perceived as incompetent and of the social consequences inherent in that perception. The threat of a devalued social identity provides a powerful incentive for maintaining both physical and social distance from people more seriously stigmatized. As Erving Goffman (1963) suggests: "In general, the tendency for a stigma to spread from the stigmatized individual . . . provides a reason why such relations tend either to be avoided or to be terminated, where existing" (p. 30).

Perhaps it is this attempt to avoid stigma by association that explains the attitude of Laura Bridgman toward mental retardation. It may also explain the phenomenon of differential advocacy as it exists today.

REFERENCES AND FURTHER READINGS

Birenbaum, A. (1970). On managing a courtesy stigma. *Journal of Health and Social Behavior, 11,* 196–206.

Birenbaum, A. (1971). The recognition and acceptance of stigma. *Sociological Symposium, 7,* 15–22.

Birenbaum, A. (1992). Courtesy stigma revisited. *Mental Retardation, 30,* 265-268.

Dickens, C. (1842). *American notes.* London: Oxford University Press.

Edgerton, R. (1967). *The cloak of competence: Stigma in the lives of the mentally retarded.* Berkeley: University of California Press.

Ellison, R. (1952). *Invisible man.* New York: Random House.

Ferguson, P. (1994). *Abandoned to their fate: Social policy and the practice toward severely retarded people in America, 1820–1920.* Philadelphia: Temple University Press.

Freeburg, E. (1992). An object of peculiar interest: The education of Laura Bridgman. *Church History, 61,* 191–205.

Gallaher, D. (1995). *Voice for the mad: The life of Dorothea Dix.* New York: The Free Press.

Gibbons, F. X. (1985). Stigma perception: Social comparison among mentally retarded persons. *American Journal of Mental Deficiency, 90,* 98–106.

Gitter, E. (1991). Charles Dickens. *Dickens Quarterly, 8,* 162–168.

Goffman, E. (1963). *Stigma: Notes on the management of spoiled identity.* Englewood Cliffs, NJ: Prentice Hall.

Howe M., & Hall, F. (1904). *Laura Bridgman: Dr. Howe's famous pupil and what he taught her.* London: Hodden & Stoughton.

Howe, S. (1893). *The education of Laura Bridgman*. Boston: Perkins Institute.

Mehta, S. I., & Farino, A. (1988). Associative stigma: Perceptions of the difficulties of college aged children of stigmatized fathers. *Journal of Social and Clinical Psychology, 7*, 192–202.

Meltzer, M. (1964). *A light in the dark: The life of Samuel Gridley Howe*. New York: Thomas Y. Crowell.

Neuberg, S. L., Smith, D. M., Hoffman, J. C., & Russell, F. J. (1994). When we observe stigmatized and "normal" individuals interacting: Stigma by association. *Personality and Social Psychology Bulletin, 20*, 196–209.

Smith, J. D. (1987). *The other voices: Profiles of women in the history of special education*. Seattle, WA: Special Child.

Smith, J. D. (1997). Construction of mental retardation and the challenge of advocacy: The different voices of Helen Keller and Burton Blatt. *Mental Retardation, 35*, 138–140.

Trent, J. (1994). *Inventing the feeble mind: A history of mental retardation in the United States*. Berkeley: University of California Press.

17

Disabilities and the Challenges of Equality

Looking Backward, Looking Forward

The Pledge of Allegiance was written in 1892 by Francis Bellamy for the quadricentennial celebration of the arrival of Columbus in America. Bellamy wrote the Pledge at the request of a committee of state school superintendents under the auspices of the National Education Association. The Pledge was intended to become part of a flag ceremony that would bring a new emphasis to the importance of the American flag to school children who were hardly a generation removed from the Civil War.

Bellamy's original draft of the Pledge read as follows: "I pledge allegiance to my Flag and to the Republic for which it stands, one nation, indivisible, with liberty, justice and equality for all" (Baer, 1992, p. 11). After further consideration, however, Bellamy deleted the word "equality." Through his conversations with members of his committee, he had arrived at the conclusion that it would be unacceptable to the state superintendents. He understood that a society that in 1892 still denied the vote and most other civil rights to women and to black people would not pledge itself to social equality.

In the decades that followed, the wording of the Pledge of Allegiance was twice amended. In 1924, the words "my Flag" were changed to "the Flag of the United States of America." In 1954, "under God" was added. With this addition, in a sense, the Pledge became both a patriotic oath and a public prayer. It is important to note, however, that more than a century after its adoption, the Pledge is still devoid of a commitment to equality (Baer, 1992, p. 33).

LOOKING BACKWARD

Francis Bellamy's cousin, Edward Bellamy, was a journalist and novelist. He was also a strident voice for social reform during the late 1800s. His most influential work was entitled *Looking Backward.* This book, originally printed in 1888, was a best-seller in the years following its publication. It was also very influential among American intellectuals at the time. In 1935, the philosopher and educator John Dewey ranked *Looking Backward* as one of the most important books published in the preceding fifty years.

Bellamy's novel is the story of Julian West, who falls into a trancelike sleep in 1887 and is awakened in the year 2000. West awakens to a United States that has no wars, no political parties, and no poverty. Each citizen is an equal shareholder in the social enterprise of the country, and all citizens have equitable and sufficient incomes. Throughout the book, Bellamy emphasizes that West finds in the year 2000 a society that is deeply committed to the equality of all of its citizens.

Julian West's guide in the new millennium world to which he has awakened is a physician, Dr. Leete. One of his most profound revelations is that people with disabilities are considered to be equal members of his society. When West expresses surprise that charity has become so prevalent in the United States of 2000, an intriguing exchange takes place between the two men.

"Charity!" repeated Dr. Leete. "Did you suppose that we consider the incapable class we are talking of objects of charity?"

"Why naturally," I said "inasmuch as they are incapable of self-support." But here the doctor took me up quickly.

"Who is capable of self-support?" he demanded. "There is no such thing in a civilized society as self-support . . . from the moment that men begin to live together, and constitute even the rudest sort of society, self-support becomes impossible. As men grow more civilized . . . a complex mutual dependence becomes the universal rule." (Bellamy, 1888, p. 178)

Dr. Leete continues his description of the fundamental equality of all people in his society, regardless of their individual needs or limitations in independence and productivity. To this, Julian asks, "How can they who produce nothing claim a share of the product as a right?" Dr. Leete answers that each generation in a society inherits most of what it knows and possesses. He asks West:

> How did you come to be possessors of this knowledge and this machinery which represents nine parts to the one contributed by yourself in the value of your product? You inherited it, did you not? And were not these others, these unfortunate and crippled brothers whom you cast out, joint inheritors, co-heirs with you? What I do not understand is, setting aside all considerations of justice or brotherly feeling toward the crippled and defective, how the workers of your day could have had any heart for their work, knowing that their children, or grandchildren, if unfortunate, would be deprived of the comforts and even necessities of life? (p. 181)

LOOKING FORWARD

Remarkable developments in molecular biology and genetic engineering are reported in the popular press almost daily. These advances in scientific knowledge and medical technology will almost certainly change the course of human history. The eradication of what are considered diseases, disorders, and defects may become a reality before the end of the new century. A critical question in this pursuit, however, may be how diseases, disorders, and defects are defined. Are disabilities, in this context, diseases, defects, or human differences? Is disability a condition to be prevented in all circumstances, or is it part of the spectrum of human variation? Depending upon the answer, what does this say about the status of people with disabilities in a democracy? What does it say about their fundamental equality as people?

The danger that people with disabilities will be further devalued as genetic intervention techniques increase is illustrated by recent remarks by James Watson. Winner of the Nobel Prize and codiscoverer of DNA, Watson was also the first director of the Human Genome Project. In his capacity as leader of the effort to map and sequence the genetic makeup of human beings, Watson also advocated careful consideration of the ethical, legal, and social implications of the project. And yet, in a 1993 article titled "Looking Forward" Watson dismissed the value of people with severe disabilities when he spoke of the decisions faced by "prospective parents when they learn that their prospective child carries a gene that would block its opportunity for a meaningful life" (p. 314). In the same article, he speaks disapprovingly of parents who do not undergo genetic testing: "So we must also face up to the ethical and practical dilemma, facing these individuals who could have undergone genetic diagnosis, but who for one reason or another declined the opportunity and later gave birth to children who must face up to lives of hopeless inequality" (p. 315). More recently, Watson spoke to the German Congress of Molecular Medicine (Lee, 1998) and condemned the eugenic philosophy that resulted in the atrocities of the Nazi era. Then, in an amazing contradiction, he advocated what might be termed "parental eugenics." He asserted that the truly relevant question for most families is whether an obvious good will come from having a child with a major handicap. From this perspective, Watson said, "seeing the bright side of being handicapped is like praising the virtues of extreme poverty" (p. 16).

Revisiting Eugenics

In *Backdoor to Eugenics* (1990), Troy Duster argued that eugenics is alive and well in our society but in a more subtle manifestation. While it is still being presented as an economic and social issue, eugenics is also being presented as a matter of parental responsibility or irresponsibility. Although less overt, eugenics in its new form may be even more powerful in its impact on the lives of people with disabilities.

The eugenicists of the nineteenth and twentieth centuries looked to evolutionary theory and Mendelian genetics for moral guidelines. They believed that evolutionary theory and science could provide models for social ethics. The failure of this approach was evidenced in the needless institutionalization of people with disabilities who were deemed to be unfit for social struggle, and in the needless sterilization of people inaccurately assessed to be the carriers of defective genes. Ultimately the moral horrors of the Holocaust evolved from this philosophy. What moral truths will prevail in the current eugenic climate?

Looking Forward to Equality

As the power of genetic science grows, so grows the importance of ethical questions about the implication of that power for human diversity. The greatest challenge for people with disabilities in this century may be that of having their lives understood within the contexts of the civic values of liberty, justice, *and* equality. This challenge, and hope, is embodied in the 1892 address that Francis Bellamy delivered during the unveiling of the Pledge of Allegiance (Baer, 1992). Perhaps borrowing a concept from his cousin Edward, he spoke of looking forward to a new age.

> We look forward. We are conscious we are in a period of transition. Ideas in education, in political economy, in social science are undergoing revisions. . . . The coming century promises to be more than ever the age of the people; an age that shall develop a greater care for the rights of the weak, and make a more solid provision for the development of each individual (p. 41)

Indeed, let us hope that we are living at the beginning of a century that is more than ever the age of the people, including people with disabilities.

REFERENCES AND FURTHER READINGS

Baer, J. (1992). *The pledge of allegiance: A centennial history, 1892–1992.* Annapolis, MD: Free State Press.

Bellamy, E. (1888). *Looking backward.* New York: Ticknor.

Duster, T. (1990). *Backdoor to eugenics.* New York: Routledge.

Lee, T. (1998, March/April). You probably won't like James Watson's ideas about us. *Ragged Edge,* 16.

Linton, S. (1988). *Claiming disability: Knowledge and identity.* New York: New York University Press.

Watson, J. (1993). Looking forward. *Gene, 135,* 309–315.

18

Diversity and Disability

Individuality and Mental Retardation

"Memories are not history. They are fragments of things and feelings that were tainted and sifted through varying prisms of present time and disposition" (Dayan, 1985, p. 1) This reflection by Yoel Dayan, the daughter of the revered Israeli patriot and statesman Moshe Dayan, offers a helpful perspective on our most treasured memories. We must keep in mind that the events and people we remember have likely been altered over the many times we have recalled them. With that caution expressed and forgiveness asked in advance, I share a memory.

A MEMORY FROM IGNACY GOLDBERG

During my doctoral studies at Teachers College, Columbia University, I was blessed with having professors who were not only scholars with great knowledge but also people of impressive character and deep compassion. One of my mentors was Ignacy Goldberg. As all great teachers do, he often shared with his students stories from his own life. One of his stories that I have frequently recalled, and perhaps altered or embellished, was of his experience working in a Midwest institution for persons with mental retardation.

Dr. Goldberg remembered that during his first days at the institution, an experienced staff member explained to him that there were actually three populations of residents living there. The three groups he described were the "retarded retarded," the "normal retarded," and the "minimally gifted." The retarded retarded were those people who needed constant care and attention. They could not survive without the help that was given to them by other people (often including help from the normal retarded and the minimally gifted). The normal retarded were those people who constituted the mainstream population of the institution. They cared for themselves for the most part and functioned in a relatively independent fashion within the institutional culture. They were also subject to being given the most basic and unpleasant chores to do. Their work was often supervised by the minimally gifted, who made sure that things ran smoothly in the wards of the institution and who occupied the upper echelon of the residential population. The minimally gifted were commonly rewarded by the institution staff for doing the things the staff was actually being paid to do. Their rewards varied from cigarettes, to special privileges, to money, and various favors. The quality of life and the standard of care for many of the other residents often depended on the abilities, sensibilities, and compassion of the minimally gifted. Dr. Goldberg discussed the degrading nature of the words used to describe the residents, particularly the sarcasm of the designation "minimally gifted." The idea behind the descriptions, however, he had found to be valid. There were distinctly different populations of people in institutions that were designed and operated for *the* retarded, a supposedly monolithic group.

I often thought of Dr. Goldberg's story as I visited residential facilities early in my own career. I believe that I have seen it played out a number of times. Recalling his descriptions of the hierarchies and population differences in institutions helped me understand some of the social dynamics and individual behavior that I observed.

JACK LONDON'S "TOLD IN THE DROOLING WARD"

A striking confirmation of Dr. Goldberg's recollection came to me recently when I stumbled onto a 1916 short story by Jack London. It was written from the perspective of a resident in a state mental retardation institution in the early twentieth century. London was an admirer of eugenics, and his philosophy included the assumption of innate human limitations of both racial and social class origins. The main character in the story, Tom, repeats several times that the institution is the right place for him, and he implies that the outside world is too complex and competitive for him. On the other hand, London has Tom explain the ways in which he is superior to others within his institutional world and how they rely on his abilities for their well-being. Tom's description of the differences among the people in the institution make the story, "Told in the Drooling Ward," a compelling reading experience for anyone interested in the sociology of institutionalization.

> Me? I'm not a drooler. I'm the assistant. I don't know what Miss Jones or Miss Kelsey could do without me. There are fifty-five low-grade droolers in this ward, and how could they ever all be fed if I wasn't around? I like to feed the droolers. They don't make much trouble. They can't. Something's wrong with most of their legs and arms and they can't talk. They are very low-grade. I can walk, and talk, and do things. You must be careful with the droolers and not feed them too fast. . . . Miss Jones says I'm an expert. When a new nurse comes I show her how to do it. It's funny watching a new nurse try to feed them. She goes at it so slow and careful that sup-pertime would be around before she finished shoving down their breakfast. Then I show her, because I'm an expert. Dr. Dalrymple says I am, and he ought to know (p. 87).

Tom goes into further detail about his special place in the hierarchy of the institution. He also divulges the fact that there are people in the institution who have been placed there because of epilepsy and he doesn't like them. He clearly thinks that they don't belong in what he calls the Home.

> But I am a high-grade feeb. Dr. Dalrymple says I am too smart to be in the Home, but I never let on. It's a pretty good place. And I don't throw fits like lots of the feebs. You see that house up there through the trees. The high-grade epilecs all live in it by them-selves. They're stuck up because they ain't ordinary feebs. They call it the clubhouse, and they say they're just as good as anyone outside, only they're sick. I don't like them much. They laugh at me, when they ain't busy throwing fits. But I don't care. . . . Low-grade epilecs are disgusting and high-grade epilecs put on airs. I'm glad I ain't an epilec. There ain't anything to them. They just talk big, that's all. (p. 88)

Tom also describes several of his fellow residents according to the etiology of their retardation. His description of the characteristics and prognosis associated with each diagnosis is interesting and, in some cases, moving.

> Do you know what a micro is? It's the kind with the little heads no bigger than your fist. They're usually droolers, and they live a long time. The hydros don't drool. They have the big heads, and they're smarter. But they never grow up. They always die. I never look at one without thinking he's going to die. Sometimes, when I'm

feeling lazy, or the nurse is mad at me, I wish I was a drooler with nothing to do and someone to feed me. But I guess I'd sooner talk and be what I am. (p. 90)

Tom was once taken from the institution by a family that wanted to adopt him. He soon discovered, however, that the family was primarily interested in him for free labor. He was worked hard and physically abused and, after a few months, he ran away from his new home and went back to the institution. Upon returning to his ward, Tom was most concerned about a particular "drooler" whom he had missed while he was away.

I walked right into the ward. There was a new nurse feeding little Albert. "Hold on," I said. "That ain't the way. Don't you see how he is twisting that left eye? Let me show you." Mebbe she thought I was a new doctor, for she just gave me the spoon, and I guess I filled little Albert up with the most comfortable meal he'd had since I went away. Droolers ain't bad when you understand them. I heard Miss Jones tell Miss Kelsey once that I had an amazing gift in handling droolers. (p. 102)

Tom fantasizes about how his life could be improved if the staff of the institution openly recognized his abilities. He believes that if he were treated fairly he could have a "normal" life in the Home.

Some day mebbe, I am going to talk with Doctor Dalrymple and get him to give me a declaration that I ain't a feeb. Then I'll get him to make me a real assistant in the drooling ward, with forty dollars a month and my board. And then I'll marry Miss Jones and live right on here. And if she won't have me, I'll marry Miss Kelsey or some other nurse. There's lots of them that want to get married. And I won't care if my wife gets mad and calls me a feeb. What's the good? And I guess when one's learned to put up with droolers, a wife won't be much worse. (p. 103)

At the end of the story, however, Tom admits that he knows that his life in the institution will not change. He also knows that he could never leave the community that needs him because he is a "high-grade" and not a drooler. He has developed relationships, especially with little Albert, that give meaning to his life. He admits that even if his dream of running away and finding work in a gold mine were to come true, he would miss the friendships and roles he has established in the Home.

Next time I run away, I am going right over that mountain. But I ain't going to take epilecs along. They ain't never cured, and when they get scared or excited they throw fits to beat the band. But I'll take little Albert. Somehow I can't get along without him. And anyway, I ain't going to run away. The drooling ward's a better snap than gold mines, and I hear there's a new nurse coming. Besides, little Albert's bigger than I am now, and I could never carry him over a mountain. (p. 107)

THE TYPOLOGY OF MENTAL RETARDATION

Typological thinking is the belief that complex individual variations can be reduced to underlying human types or essences. Stephen Gelb (1997) has found that definitions of mental retardation, regardless of their particulars, are grounded in typological thought. The core of mental retardation as a field is the assumption that somehow there is a "mental retardation essence" that eclipses all of the differences that characterize people described by the term. Ignacy Goldberg's story of people who are retarded retarded, normal retarded, and minimally gifted contradicts this sense of a single essence of retardation. Tom's description of droolers, feebs, epilecs, micros, and hydros also illustrates how people with various disabilities or life conditions have been both literally and figuratively aggregated under the same term—*mentally retarded*.

Even a brief glance at the panoply of etiologies associated with mental retardation illustrates the allure and power of typological thinking. In 1992, the American Association on Mental Retardation listed more than three hundred and fifty conditions in which mental retardation occurs. This list of causes does not, of course, take into account the varying degrees of retardation or other disabilities associated with each of the etiologies. When those variables are taken into account, the universe of human conditions subsumed under the term *mental retardation* is staggering. The only "glue" that holds mental retardation together as a category is the typological notion that there is some underlying and shared essence to the characteristics and needs of the people identified by the term. Clearly mental retardation is an aggregate of human conditions.

MENTAL RETARDATION: REDEFINING OR DISAGGREGATING?

Perhaps it is time to abandon mental retardation as a classification, rather than continuing the quest for a more humane or more scientific definition of the term. Mental retardation and its various definitions are, in fact, manifestations of the typological thinking that inevitably creates a simplistic and misleading aggregation of people with very diverse needs and characteristics.

There must be alternatives for conceptualizing the needs of the people currently referred to as having mental retardation. It may be helpful to ask ourselves questions about what the abandonment of the term and the definitions associated with it could mean in the lives of individuals and families. We must also ask ourselves what abandoning mental retardation as a classification might mean for resource allocations and the provisions of services to people who need them. Finally, we must consider the impact of the deconstruction of retardation in terms of need versus stigma. In other words, is the aggregation of people into this diagnostic category truly necessary to meet their needs? Are services in the name of mental retardation justified given the risk of stigma associated with the label? How can we provide for those who need assistance without diminishing their identity and integrity as individuals? These are questions that seem to be critical in giving thought to the dismantling of the concept.

The time is overdue, however, for a fundamental questioning of the terms and practices associated with retardation. The millions of people with developmental disabilities who have been subsumed under that classification deserve a careful analysis of its impact on the manner in which they are regarded and treated. A careful consideration of the feasibility of disassembling the aggregation that mental retardation has become may enhance our vision of what it should be.

REFERENCES AND FURTHER READINGS

Dayan, Y. (1985). *My father, his daughter.* London: Weidenfield & Nicholson.

Gelb, S. (1997). The problem of typological thinking in mental retardation. *Mental Retardation, 35,* 448–457.

Labor, E., & Reesman, J. (1994). *Jack London.* New York: Twayne.

London, J. (1916). "Told in the drooling ward." In *The turtles of Tasman.* New York: Macmillan.

Luckasson, R., Coulter, D. L., Polloway, E. A., Reiss, S., Shalock, L.L., Snell, M. E., Spitalnik, D. M., & Stark, J. A. (1992). *Mental retardation: Definition, classification, and systems or supports.* Washington, DC: American Association on Mental Retardation.

Part III
Questions to Ponder

1. How can the apparent contradiction between Darwin's personal and scientific attitudes toward disability be explained? Can you think of other literary or historical examples of this contradiction? Can you think of examples from your own experience?

2. Is the approach to disability described by Margaret Mead possible in a large and complex society like the United States? Why?

3. How does the attitude of Laura Bridgman toward mental retardation compare to Helen Keller's attitude as described in Part II? Why?

4. Is the utopian inclusiveness described by Bellamy possible? Why?

5. Do you agree or disagree that *mental retardation* is a term and concept that should be abandoned? Why?

Epilogue

Finding a Voice: The Story of Bill

The following story was told to me by one of my professors when I was a student preparing to become a teacher. It is about one of his former students. The story has strengthened and sustained my belief in the critical difference that one teacher can make in the life of a student. It has served to remind me for many years now of the importance of hope, sensitivity, and innovation in the work that we do as teachers. I have shared this story with generations of my own students, and I am pleased to share it with you.

Amy, a special education major at a small college, had reached her senior year. She told her advisor that she very much wanted to do her student teaching in a nearby residential facility for adults with mental retardation operated by the state. Amy explained that she preferred that kind of placement to student teaching in a public school. Her career goal was to teach adults with mental retardation. And so her adviser, later my professor, made the arrangements. Amy had also requested that she be assigned to work with people with more severe disabilities. Accordingly, she was given a small number of people with multiple disabilities to work with on an individual basis. She was assigned four people to develop and implement programs for during the fifteen-week period of her student teaching.

One of the men she was assigned to work with was thirty-five years old. He had severe cerebral palsy and had been diagnosed as being severely mentally retarded. He was in a wheelchair. He had no control over the movement of his legs. He had some voluntary movement in his arms, but he could not control them very well. He was also able to move some of the muscles in his neck and face. He could not, however, speak. The assumption noted in his records was that he was unable to speak because of his retardation. But something about this man, whose name was Bill, gave Amy the impression there was more within him than had been recognized. There was something about the way he moved his eyes, she said. There was something about the way he seemed to react to the things she said to him. She was told by people who worked at the facility that Bill loved being read to. One person commented, "We don't think he understands anything, but he just loves to hear the sound of a voice reading to him." She tried it and, sure enough, he did react very positively the minute he saw the book in her hand. "His eyes brightened up," she said.

Bill had been in the institution since he was an infant, having been brought there by his parents, who felt that they could not take care of him. Amy decided, "Here's a man who has no way of communicating. The only semblance of communication we have is when I watch his face, like when I bring a book into the room and his eyes seem to light up." She later reflected, "I didn't know what that meant—his eyes lighting up. I just wanted to find some way of beginning to teach him to communicate."

In college, Amy had learned about communication boards and how they can be helpful to people who are unable to speak. This was before the development of the various computer keyboards, voice synthesizers, and other augmentative devices that have become so important today in enabling people with disabilities to communicate. But Amy's professors had encouraged her to be resourceful and creative. So, she made a very simple communication board one evening after work. She took a big square of cardboard, divided it into four sections, and put a picture in each section. In one section she put a picture of a glass of orange juice, in another section a picture of a bathroom door, in the third section a picture of a book, and in the last section a picture of a park bench and a tree. Bill had enough movement in his arms and hands to point to these pictures, and she wanted to teach him that if he wanted a drink of orange juice, his favorite drink, he should point to the glass of orange juice on the board. If he needed to use the bathroom, she wanted to teach him that he could point to the picture of the bathroom door, and so on. She brought the board in and demonstrated it to him. Amy placed his hand on the picture of the tree and then she took him outside to the bench, a special place, it seemed, for Bill. She came back inside and put his hand on the picture of the book and then opened a book and read to him. In the process, she thought, "I'll try this for several days and see if I can get him to catch on."

Bill's response, however, proved to be immediate. Amy finished reading and was going to take his hand and point to the glass of orange juice, but he shook his head and grunted. She wasn't sure, but it seemed that he wanted her to continue reading.

She read a few more pages and Bill seemed pleased. When she placed the communication board on his wheelchair again, Bill pointed first to the book and then to the bench. She corrected him by placing his finger on only one of the pictures, the bench. When she gave him another trial, however, he repeated the sequence of touching the book and the bench. She wasn't certain, but she thought that perhaps he was trying to say he wanted them to go outside and read the book. She pushed his wheelchair toward the exit door, and as they passed through it she thought she heard Bill giggle with delight.

That night Amy made a larger communication board with more pictures and thus more alternatives. What she saw from Bill the next day was immediate comprehension of how to use the bigger board. She then decided to make a communication board with all the letters of the alphabet, thinking maybe she could begin teaching him to spell words. She brought it to work and began using it by trying to teach him the word *book*. She felt that his love of being read to might motivate him to learn *book* as his first word. She held his finger and pointed to B, then to O, to another O, and finally to K. She repeated the word *book* and put his hand on the one she had been reading from. She then encouraged Bill to point to the letters on his own. His finger went immediately to the letter T. She corrected him by placing his finger again on the B and calling out the name of the letter. When he was again given the freedom to point, however, his finger went in a seemingly deliberate manner to the T. Amy decided to let him proceed. Bill in a slow, labored and careful way, pointed to the sequence of letters that communicated to her his message of choice. He said to his teacher, T H A N K   Y O U. Amy was astounded.

Bill had never been taught to read or write; he had never had academic instruction of any kind. Apparently, however, over the years when people read to him, Bill watched carefully. He had taught himself to read. Amy began to work with Bill on the communication board with great intensity. She spent her evenings and weekends listening to him through his pointing to letters. He spoke with her about a lifetime of unexpressed perceptions and silent frustrations. Once she understood how deeply he could communicate using the spelling board, she told others at the institution. Many of them said, "There must be some misunderstanding. Bill is severely retarded." She finally convinced a psychologist to watch as she asked questions of Bill, to which he responded by pointing to the letters of the alphabet. The psychologist was absolutely amazed. He decided to give Bill some sections of an IQ test through his communication board. Not only did he find that Bill was not severely mentally retarded, the psychologist estimated that his IQ fell into the superior range. He had been locked into his body for thirty-five years and treated as if he were severely retarded. He had no way of telling the world he wasn't. Amy had given him a key—she had given him a means of communicating and demonstrating the depth of his comprehension and insight.

By this time, Amy was nearing the completion of her student teaching. She asked special permission, however, to remain at the facility that summer and work with Bill. This was allowed. As a result of Amy's efforts and the world that had opened to him through the communication board, Bill moved out of the institution the next year and into a group home.

Amy continued to work with him and taught him to type on an electric typewriter. It was a slow process, but he mastered it. A new freedom of expression came to him with the keyboard.

Bill developed friendships in the community that surrounded the group home. He became an active member of a local church. He loved going to community theater performances. He was invited to join a civic organization. Unfortunately, he died of a stroke when he was in his late forties. It is sad to think that until he was thirty-five years old he was treated as severely disabled by everyone who knew him. He had so few years of liberation from his disability. His friend and teacher, Amy, however, found a way of helping him break through, so that for at least ten years of his life he was recognized as a person, not as a disability.

We all need to be very careful with the assumptions we make about people, and extremely careful about the assumptions we make about people who have trouble communicating. We often jump to conclusions when people can't communicate effectively, and we sometimes have lower expectations of them. Bill and Amy come to my mind when I am tempted to make judgments about the potentials of others. I'm glad Bill found a voice. I'm glad that I know their story. I hope that in sharing this story we are all reminded that the most disabling handicaps are created when our misperceptions and misunderstandings place stereotypes where insights on our shared humanity are most needed.

Index

**CORWIN
PRESS**

The Corwin Press logo—a raven striding across an open book—represents the happy union of courage and learning. We are a professional-level publisher of books and journals for K-12 educators, and we are committed to creating and providing resources that embody these qualities. Corwin's motto is "Success for All Learners."